· THE ·
WELL-ORDERED
HOME

*Organizing Techniques for
Inviting Serenity into Your Life*

Kathleen Kendall-Tackett, Ph.D.

New Harbinger Publications, Inc.

Publisher's Note

This publication is designed to provide accurate and authoritative information in regard to the subject matter covered. It is sold with the understanding that the publisher is not engaged in rendering psychological, financial, legal, or other professional services. If expert assistance or counseling is needed, the services of a competent professional should be sought.

Distributed in the U.S.A. by Publishers Group West; in Canada by Raincoast Books; in Great Britain by Hi Marketing, Ltd.; in South Africa by Real Books, Ltd.; in Australia by Boobook; and in New Zealand by Tandem Press.

Cover design by Amy Shoup
Edited by Carole Honeychurch
Text design by Michele Waters

ISBN 1-57224-321-X Paperback

Printed in the United States of America

New Harbinger Publications' Web site address: www.newharbinger.com

05   04   03

10   9   8   7   6   5   4   3   2   1

First printing

Contents

Welcome to the
Well-Ordered Home

Congratulations! You are about to embark on a life-changing adventure. To enter a time when you can always find your car keys, always have something clean to wear, and never run out of toilet paper. Where you have time to be with your family and friends and can curl up with a good book, take a long walk, or enjoy a Sunday afternoon nap. Sound impossible? It's not.

You may believe that organized homes belong to boring people who need to get a life. Nothing could be further from the truth. A well-ordered home simply *works*. People get to where they need to be, tasks get done, family life is cherished, all with a minimum amount of fuss and bother. Because, when organization is done well, it fades into the background, *allowing* you to have a life.

Let's consider the flip side. Can disorganization be bad? You tell me. Life is substantially more stressful when chaos reigns. Stuff gets lost. You're always behind. You end up taking longer to do the same amount of work. And people are always mad at you—or at least, annoyed. In short, there is a connection between mess and stress.

My Story

Allow me to introduce myself. I'm a health psychologist and researcher at the University of New Hampshire. I write, lecture, and talk to people about stress. And as you probably already know, household chores are a major source of stress. I've seen this firsthand. While in school, I also cleaned houses, sold kitchen supplies, and worked as a home health aide. Those jobs gave me license to open drawers, root around in cupboards, and look under sinks. I've had an intimate glimpse into a wide range of homes and have seen what works and what doesn't.

Organization has also been a personal odyssey. After my second son was born, I needed to bring more order to my home life, and I eventually did. The suggestions I share here were tested in the real world. I have two sons, a dog, three cats, and quite a few hamsters (that's another story!). My house is not minimalist. There are often projects out on tables. At first glance, it may not seem "orderly." But as you spend time with us, you'll see that order is there. When things get busy (and they always do), my home does not fall apart. Life goes on with a minimum of stress.

Four Key Principles for Household Organization

There are four key principles to keep in mind. These are simple to apply and can work in almost any situation.

- **Start Where You Are.** Don't make change a prerequisite for organization. Start where you are and work with strengths you already have.

- **Have What You Need.** As a culture, we are inundated with stuff. Yet often we don't have what we need to work well. This book will make sure you do.

- **Use Active Storage.** In this book, I'll introduce you to the concept of active storage. Active storage means keeping things you use frequently in accessible areas. I'll show you how to do that in every area of your home.

- **Get Rid of Clutter.** Clutter creates stress and makes every job more difficult. In this book, I'll offer you specific suggestions for keeping what you value and getting rid of the excess.

So come along with me, and we'll bring more beauty, order, and joy to your home. Don't you deserve it?

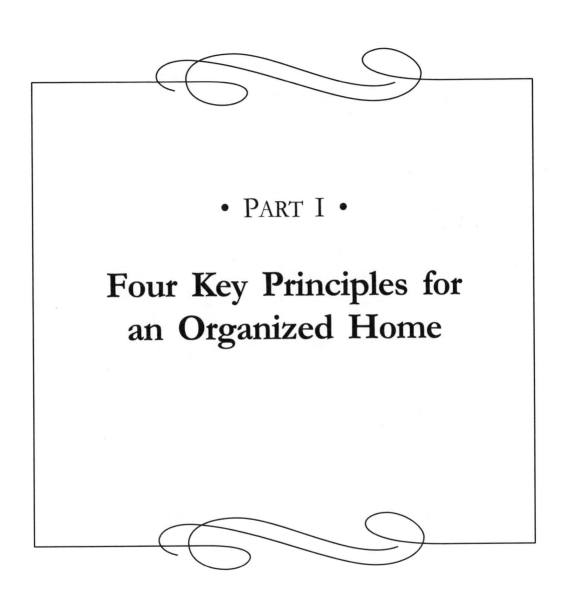

• PART I •

Four Key Principles for an Organized Home

• 1 •
Start Where You Are

I often find myself in the role of priest, as people share their guilty confessions of household disorder. Underlying these confessions are a lot of "shoulds." You may have similar confessions to make. You might try to be more disciplined, thinking that if you just buy the right organizer, home office setup, or storage device, you'll land at the magical destination of "organized."

Instead of trying to force a change, I propose that you start where you are. This means working with your natural bent and approaching household tasks knowing who you are and how you like to do things. Conversely, *not* starting where you are means fighting against yourself, making any task more difficult. Here are some examples.

What Happens When You Don't

You set up a great home office that is fully equipped with everything you need—office supplies, a place to file, a brand-new "in-basket"—but it's far away from your front door. Even though you resolve to sort your mail at your desk, you never do because you come home tired and don't want to trek that far. So you leave the mail on the kitchen counter. From there, it ends up stacked or scattered throughout the house.

Or you buy an electronic organizer with all the bells and whistles, thinking that it will finally get you organized. But you're not really comfortable with electronic devices. You never enter the information you need, but drag it around with you because you paid a lot for it. Instead, you use the paper date book that cost a dollar at the drug store.

How to Start Where You Are

The mistake made in both of these situations was trying to use a tool or system that wasn't right for you. Don't make change a prerequisite for getting organized. Instead, ask yourself the following questions.

- How do I prefer to do things?

- What skills and equipment do I already possess?

- Am I trying to force myself to do something?

For example, recognize that it is unlikely that you will train yourself to come into your home a different way. So set up the entrance you *do* use to store your keys, coat, and gear you brought with you for the day. Going back to our examples, recognize that you are often too tired to go all the way to your desk, and that no home office, no matter how nicely put together, will entice you to go there when you come home. So set up the area that you *do* hang around in to process mail and keep track of your calendar.

If you are a technophobe (or even just leery of technology), don't force yourself to use a piece of equipment, be it a computer or an electronic organizer. If you're already having trouble getting started, having an intimidating piece of equipment is just going to make procrastination that much easier.

Next time you get stuck, ask yourself whether you're starting where you are. In almost every case, the answer to any organizational dilemma will come by working with, rather than against, your natural bent.

• 2 •

Have What You Need

Having what you need helps you beat procrastination by making it easier for you to do the task you need to get done. Otherwise, despite your good intentions, you might notice that something is dirty and think "That's dirty. I should clean that." But it could be days, or even weeks, before you get to it. On the other hand, if your cleaning supplies are right there, you can take care of it when you notice it. Since it's easier to clean up these little messes, you may do it more often, avoiding having to clean up huge messes later on. So, practically, what does this mean? It means keeping your tools and supplies where you're most likely to use them.

What Do You Need?

Here are some guidelines on what's most efficient to keep in each area.

General Household Cleaning Supplies

Each room in your home should have a trash can. A duster and spray cleaner should also be handy for each floor of your home. Similarly, keep vacuums near where you need them. If you live in a multistory house, you might consider a vacuum for each floor. Premoistened wipes can be handy for areas that need cleaning but are not near a sink. Keep a supply of light bulbs near where you have lights, especially any specialty lights such as those for a bathroom vanity or dining-area fixture. When you notice that one is burned out, you can replace it. Otherwise, you may stare at a burned out bulb for weeks.

Bathroom Supplies

Keep a caddy of cleaning supplies in each bathroom. These include paper towels and rags, cleanser for the toilet, sink, and shower, glass cleaner and squeegees, a toilet brush, and plunger. Keep extra toilet paper handy too (your guests will thank you).

Car

I keep cleaning supplies for my car in my car. I also have a trash can in my garage, so I can grab any trash out of my car and dump it before it even gets into my house.

Pet Supplies

Pet-grooming products, such as brushes or nail clippers, can be kept where you and your pets tend to congregate (where you watch TV is often a good place).

Office Supplies

Keeping a small stash of office supplies (stamps, return-address labels, envelopes) in my kitchen has been very handy. When I need to mail something, I can do so immediately without having to trek upstairs to my office. That's just one fewer thing lying around, running the risk of getting lost.

Thank-you notes (remember those?) are easier to do when I keep a few handy. I don't always get to these, but it's worth doing. I'm much more likely to write a quick note if I have some note cards at hand.

As you find out how practical this strategy is, you may apply it to other tasks. I've recently been painting my upstairs bathroom. This is a large job, since there are four doorways and many angled walls. I've been able to work on this in the little bits of time I have free by keeping all my painting supplies handy. When I have a spare hour, I can be ready to paint in just a few minutes.

In short, having what you need makes any task easier and more pleasant. Try it. I think you'll like it.

• 3 •
Use Active Storage

Active storage is a principle I learned from the old time-and-motion studies. These studies examined, in minute detail, how people worked on assembly lines. The authors then made specific recommendations on how workspaces should be set up to increase efficiency. Active storage is one of those strategies. At its crux is the idea that not everything you store needs to be equally accessible. With active storage, items you use frequently go in the front, on low shelves, and in the middle. Items you use less often go toward the back, up high, and maybe even in a different area of your home. This approach is useful anytime I start feeling really tight on space, whether it's in my desk drawers, closet, or kitchen cabinets. Here's how it works.

Active Kitchen Storage

In your kitchen, you should be able to immediately lay your hands on your pot holders, kitchen towels, paring knives, cutting boards, spoons and whisks, and your salt and pepper—items you use every day (although your list may look somewhat different). To get to these, you shouldn't have to paw through the roaster you use twice a year, serving bowls that you got as wedding presents, and the various kitchen gadgets that you use only occasionally.

Active storage can do wonders for your kitchen organization and can make even a tiny kitchen work well. By keeping handy the items you use frequently, you can make the most of the storage space that you have. Drawers, in particular, are prime real estate in a kitchen. I can't tell you the number of times that I've opened a drawer and seen it stuffed with coupons, recipes, and other stuff that I know is not being used every day. Try to reserve easily accessible drawer space for items you use all the time. Also, try to think about what activity you do in each area of your kitchen, whether it's food prep, cooking on the stove, or washing dishes. Have the things you need for those tasks in your active storage space. Keep your cutting boards, knives, and colanders near your prep area. Keep your soap, dish rags, and drying rack near your sink. Keep your pots and pans, pot holders, and stirring spoons near your stove.

Active Storage in Your Closet

Clothing that currently fits you and is appropriate for the season goes in the middle of your closet and in your drawers. The stuff that doesn't fit, or that's not appropriate for the season goes off to the sides or in the back. If closet space is at a premium, completely move seasonal clothing out of this space. Do the same for clothing that doesn't fit. If you have a little more room, keep these things in the closet, but move them to the ends or the less-accessible space. Make it your goal to be able to reach in and grab what you need without having to sort through everything else.

Active storage will reduce or even eliminate "pawing and thrashing"—that time when you are rooting around like an animal. It will shave time off of everything you do. Rather than wasting the hours each week the average American blows searching for lost items, the things you need will be at hand. Soon you will find that you're saving hours each week—time I'm sure you could put to better use.

Now that you've been introduced to active storage, what could be rearranged

- in your kitchen?

- in your bedroom?

- in your bathroom?

- in your garage?

• 4 •
Get Rid of Clutter

Americans have too much stuff, and this is perhaps the biggest impediment to becoming more organized. Clutter often accumulates just out of habit. Our homes are like the Dead Sea: having only an inlet, but no outlet. We bring stuff home, and it never leaves. We replace something that is broken or that we don't like, and keep both. We have stuff that we (or our kids) have outgrown, and we hang on to it.

Preparing to Dejunk

Take a serious look around, and answer these questions.

- Do you see anything that you no longer use?

- Are there items that are broken? If so, can they be fixed, or do they need to be replaced or even eliminated?

- Are there items that someone else can use?

- Do you have clothing in four different sizes in your closet? (We'll talk about your closet more in later chapters.)

Clutter can dramatically increase the time you spend in any task. It takes longer to clean if every surface is covered with knickknacks and your rooms are overflowing with furniture. Working in a crammed kitchen is unpleasant and wastes our time. Trying to put clothes away in a too-full dresser drawer is a pain. Adding more toys to the three-foot mound is frustrating. If you've been applying the principle of active storage, you may already have some ideas about which items can go.

Forget What You've Heard

"If you haven't used it in a year, get rid of it." I'm sure you're familiar with that organization canard. These types of hard-and-fast rules are well-intended, but pretty brainless. And this rule does not apply to many items like mementos from your childhood, your wedding dress (when was the last time you wore *that* puppy?), or pictures of your children. Even tools and other nonmementos would not fit under this rule. Before chucking items you own, ask yourself some questions about each thing.

- If you put it in a handier place, would you use it?

- Are you missing something you need in order to use it? Can you get what you need so that the item is usable?

- Is it obsolete for you? If so, could someone else make use of it? (A lot of computer equipment fits under this category.)

As you start clearing debris from your life, give yourself credit for having a brain and using it. If you notice that you have made some unwise purchases (and we all have), become aware of that, resolve to do better next time, and then *let it go*.

Start considering some of the stuff you can live without. It can be furniture, books, music and videos, clothing, kitchen tools, paper, and even habits. Going through what you own can be wonderfully freeing. You'll save time and be able to share some of your abundance with others. You can't go wrong.

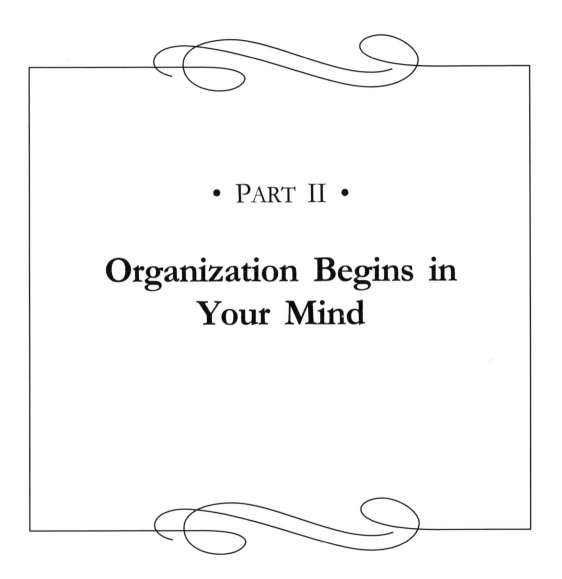

• PART II •

Organization Begins in Your Mind

• 5 •
Thinking Matters:
Thoughts That Sabotage Organization

Household organization—and disorganization—begins in your mind. That means your efforts to put your house in order are often sabotaged by the way you think about them. The good news is that once you recognize some of these likely pitfalls, you can overcome them.

Traps to Avoid

Below are some of the most common hazards you may encounter.

Perfectionism. Perfectionists put things off until they can do them "perfectly." I've seen this taken to an absurd degree. People will have their house literally coming down around their ears and will refuse to organize if they can't do things "just right." Realize that it's unlikely that anything in your home will ever be perfect. All you can do is your best, and that will certainly be better than where you are now.

All-or-nothing thinking. This belief is a first cousin of perfectionism. It's the idea that if you can't do everything now, you won't do anything. It mocks any of your efforts to take small steps. But, as I describe in chapter 7, small steps make a difference. You may not be able to tackle everything at once, but your home didn't get into its current state overnight either. Remember, each step is progress toward your goal.

Feeling that domestic work is not worth your time. In our culture, we are deeply ambivalent toward domestic activity. On one hand, we claim that it's not worth our time, that "smart" or "successful" people don't bother with it. On the other hand, we have made Martha Stewart one of the richest women in the world. I hope by the end of this book that I can convince you that household organization *is* worth your time. Yes, you may be able to hire some of the work out, including hiring an organizer. But even if you do this, *you* still have to make final decisions about what gets done. A messy house costs you money and causes stress. In contrast, an inviting home blesses everyone who enters it—including you.

What Can Help

Once you recognize the thoughts that are defeating your efforts, you can take some steps to improve them.

- **Recognize them.** The first step is to recognize, and perhaps verbalize, these unhelpful beliefs. As you become more familiar with these unhelpful beliefs, you'll recognize them more quickly.

- **Challenge them with truth.** Ask yourself whether these unhelpful thoughts are really true. For example, does everything have to be perfect to be worthwhile?

- **Address the difficulties.** If you notice that you are prone to a certain pattern of negative thinking, recognize it and take some steps to counter it. For example, if you tend toward all-or-nothing thinking, start small and create pockets of organization within your household. Pretty soon, you will be able to see compelling evidence that your efforts are making a difference.

Recognizing and dealing with thoughts that sabotage your efforts can bring you closer to having an organized home. And recognizing self-defeating thoughts will help you in other areas of life as well.

• 6 •
Strategies to Bust Procrastination

Authors are often black-belt procrastinators. We say—and truly believe—that we want to write. But give us a free day and a blank computer screen, and suddenly we've got twenty other things to do. Just today, I was convinced that I couldn't start writing until I cleaned my exercise ball. Why do we do this? Because writing is hard and often lonely work. In fact, it bears a lot of resemblance to getting your house in order. But even as proficient procrastinators, most writers have learned how to make themselves work. If you procrastinate, here are some strategies that will help.

Give yourself a time limit. This is a time-honored way to bust procrastination. Tell yourself that you only have to do the task for some specific, limited amount of time. Fifteen minutes is often a good amount. Limiting a job to fifteen minutes makes it seem more doable. No, you probably won't finish it in that amount of time. But working at even a very big job for bits and pieces of time will eventually get it done. And what frequently happens is that you get into it, decide it's not so bad, and work longer.

Time yourself doing it. A lot of time, we fuss over a job that we don't want to do because we think (often erroneously) that it will take a long time. We often spend much more time dreading a task than it actually takes to do it. If you time yourself, you may discover that a job you hate only takes you five minutes to do.

My morning oatmeal takes two minutes to cook in the microwave. I'm always amazed at how much I can do in those two minutes. I can load or unload most of the dishwasher, make a pot of tea, or tidy and wipe down the counters. Time yourself doing a job you generally avoid. You'll probably be in for a pleasant surprise.

Make it easy to do. Tasks are more likely to get done if they are easy. Make sure you have the materials you need to do them and that they are accessible. Next time you find yourself procrastinating about a task, ask yourself why. Is it because it's hard to do? If so, can you make it easier?

Get some help. We sometimes procrastinate because we don't want to work alone, especially all day. If that's the case for you, get a family member or friend to help. Remember to do the same for them.

Always have a "Plan B." Sometimes we get all fired up to do something and we run into a problem. It's so easy to give up here. But I've learned that if I always have a Plan B, I can keep the momentum going. If I can't do one thing, I do another. If one technique doesn't work, I try something else. If you go through life inflexibly thinking that you have to do things in a certain order, you're going to be frustrated a lot of the time—and pretty inefficient too.

Beating procrastination will take you a long way toward your goal. And if all else fails, just tell yourself that you have to write. You'll be amazed at the amount of cleaning you get done!

• 7 •
Little Steps Mean a Lot

I recently read a famous author's memoir. Throughout this book, he shared some of his secrets of being a successful writer. One of them was consistent work on a book; he wrote ten pages every day. To me, ten pages hardly seemed like anything. How could he be so productive with such a small number? He answered me in the very next sentence. At a rate of ten pages a day, he had fifty pages in a week. In a period of ten weeks, he had five-hundred manuscript pages. Suddenly, ten pages a day seemed like quite a lot.

I read this at a good time. I was in the early stages of writing a book that I knew was going to be mammoth, and between you and me, I was having a hard time getting started. (Having just finished it, I can tell you that I was right to be scared.) The task seemed overwhelming because the project was so large. The author's advice brought me back to an important principle: little steps mean a lot. By working consistently, bit by bit, I could accomplish a big project.

And so it is for organizing. Organizing your household may be on your list of thing to do, right next to "lose weight," "exercise," or "eat more vegetables." You might be waiting until you have a "block of time." Realistically, that block will probably never appear. But you already know that.

Right now, the idea of "getting organized" may seem so large, so impossible, so overwhelming that you don't even know where to begin. If you feel that way, I want to assure you that little steps can add up to a big difference in your life. As, little by little, you get more on top of things, you'll find that time blocks start opening up. And the effects of organizing can be synergestic. You may get so excited about the results of what you have accomplished that you're inspired to do even more.

Here are some specific suggestions to help get you started.

- Start by picking *one* task that you have been avoiding or that makes your daily work take more time.

- Resolve to spend a short amount of time on it every day (even ten to fifteen minutes).

- Gather whatever tools you will need ahead of time and keep them easily accessible for whenever you actually feel like organizing.

- Silence that voice in your head that keeps distracting you with all the *other* tasks you need to complete.

- Concretely reward yourself for progress that you make along the way.

Remember, each minute that you don't have to spend thrashing around for things can be used more effectively somewhere else. That may not sound like a lot, but over time it can really add up. For example, if you managed to save ten minutes a day in your daily routine, by the end of the week you will have saved seventy minutes—more than an hour. By the end of the year, you'll have saved sixty-one hours! And chances are it will be even more. This is because once you start freeing up time, other parts of your life will get more organized, saving you even more time. Think of it as the magic of compound interest—only applied to time.

Getting organized can be one of the most liberating things you do. Start with some simple steps and see how far you can go!

• 8 •
Why Is Organization So Hard?

Anyplace I go, people tell me they are having trouble staying on top of the details of their lives. In fact, it's harder to be organized than it was even a generation ago because more stuff comes into your life on a daily basis. Here is what I mean.

Paper. Each day, you handle about 300 sheets of paper, including catalogs, magazines, newspapers, junk mail, and school papers. In a year, the average American handles 660 pounds of paper—roughly *six times* more than in 1950. The computer was supposed to end all this dependence on paper. Ha! If anything, it has increased the amount of paper you process.

Time. Americans now have the longest work week of any industrialized nation, and much of this time is spent away from our homes. When forced to choose between family and household debris, household debris usually loses (and rightly so, in my view). However, the net result is that you fall further and further behind.

More house. The size of American houses has doubled. In the 1950s, the average home was 900 square feet. The average new home is nearly twice that size. Filling all that lovely space results in more to take care of and tend to.

Shop till you drop. The mass-market availability of cheap goods, onslaught of nonstop advertising, and easy availability of credit has turned us into a nation of shoppers. How do you organize when you can't even get the drawer closed?

What Can Help

If these problems sound familiar, take heart. You have lots of company. But even with today's crazy schedule and avalanche of stuff, you can bring order to your home.

- **Stop paper from stacking up.** Get in the habit of sorting through your paper every day, including mail, newspapers, and schoolwork. Set up a paper-recycling bin and designate a place to sort your mail. This will keep your stacks from growing any bigger.

- **Rethink your activities.** If you are swamped, see if there are any activities you can eliminate or reduce. Once you are even a little less harried, your house may begin to be easier to manage.

- **Too much house.** This can actually be an advantage. It is often easier to be more organized when you have extra space. Just resist the temptation to fill all your spaces with extras you don't need.

- **Curtail shopping.** One wonderful byproduct of bringing your home under control is that you become more appreciative of stuff you already own. That tends to limit shopping.

There are real obstacles to household organization. Knowing this, you can stop assuming guilt for things that are not your fault and channel your energies more effectively.

• 9 •

Nurture Your Inner Scientist

Children are natural scientists. They love to experiment, make adjustments, or do things in a different way. They are open to trying something new. If that doesn't work, they try something else.

Somewhere along the way, children lose that ability. They grow into adults who have responsibilities and things they need to do. They stop experimenting and lose that sense of wonder and adventure. Everything is so serious. So intense. So earnest. They give up experimenting.

Many of the tasks we hate are drudgery. They may be boring, physically challenging, or involve handling nasty things. We dread these activities, often with very good reason. There is so much to do, and little time to do it in. We don't have a chance to think about doing things differently. Experimenting is too much like *play,* and we don't have time for that!

The Importance of Play

I'm going to suggest that a little play is exactly what you need. Part of bringing our households into order is being willing to experiment with different ways of doing things. Instead of living on autopilot, I'm going to encourage you to nurture that inner scientist. Bring back your childlike wonder and curiosity. Be open to experimenting with new things. Here are some suggestions.

- **Scrutinize your routines.** Examine all the things you do around your home and ask yourself whether there is a way to do them better, faster, or more efficiently.

- **Put yourself in the role of learner.** Don't expect to know everything. Give yourself permission to learn. When someone you know has a good way of doing things, ask her about it. Find a pro, and ask how he does it.

- **Try different methods of doing things.** Is this cleaning product effective, or is there one that might work better? Is it better for you to sit or stand? If you don't know which technique is more effective for a certain type of job, try a couple of them and see which one works best for you.

- **Time yourself doing a job.** See if you can do it faster.

- **Try different times of day.** Do you work better in the morning or the evening?

- **Try changing routines.** Is it easier for you to open your mail at the kitchen counter or in your living room? Are you more likely to hang up your coat if there is a peg than if you must use a hanger?

By nurturing your inner scientist, you may suddenly find that work you dreaded becomes more agreeable. And while you may never *love* cleaning the toilet (I live with three males—I know what I'm talking about here), perhaps it can become less odious. Next time you find yourself dreading a task, try to figure out how to make it more fun. Once you open yourself up to new ways to handle your daily work, you're on your way to having an organized home.

• 10 •
Take Advantage of the Seasons

Not long ago, human activity was governed by the seasons. Life had its own rhythms. There were times of strenuous activity and times of rest. These were automatically built into daily life. Over the last century, we've lost much of our sense of seasonal variations. And yet, even with all our technological distractions, there is still a pull of seasonal rhythms. I suggest that you try using the seasons to your advantage. Big jobs are so much easier when you actually *feel* like doing them. If you try tackling household organization by seasons, suddenly the tasks are much more manageable. Here are some ideas.

Spring

Spring is the season of renewal. The bleak days of winter give way to warmth. Everything seems lighter, brighter, more intense. It's no accident that the period of intense cleaning is called "spring cleaning." We have more energy. Sunlight streaming through our windows highlights areas in our home that need attention. Spring is a natural time to sort through winter clothing, to pare away excess that accumulated during winter, and do deep cleaning.

Summer

Summer is about warm, lazy days. Life moves at a slower pace in the summer. Kids are out of school. There are fewer places that we need to be. We cook outdoors and maybe enjoy a baseball game. Summer can also be a perfect time to tackle a big project, like organizing the family photographs, putting in a garden, or sorting through "the pile." The longer days also lend themselves to chores outside, such as home maintenance, that are easy to put off in the cooler months.

Fall

Fall is also a time of new beginnings, especially for families: new school year, new teachers, new clothes. The pace quickens. Days grow shorter. Families are once again subsumed in daily rhythms of school, car pools, sports, lessons, and homework. Schedules are key during this time. Learning to be proactive in scheduling can save considerable time.

Fall also seems to be the season of clothing. Clothing is sorted and decisions are made about what is needed and what can be passed along. Summer clothes are stored and winter clothing is once again put into action. The holiday season looms large during the fall. Much of the planning, purchasing, wrapping, and sending takes place in autumn. This is a great time to organize your gift-wrapping supplies.

Winter

The days grow shorter, the nights longer. The hectic holiday season is over. Cold weather brings people indoors. In nature, winter is a time of hibernation. For people, winter is a time to draw inward. But activity can still take place. Winter can be a time of preparation: for spring, for taxes, for emergencies. This might be a good time to develop a filing system or to gather your financial records. Take advantage of those holiday clearance sales for gift giving throughout the year. Finally, winter is a time of New Year's resolutions. Let one of yours be to have a more orderly home.

Organizing by season gives you a natural boost of energy and immediately breaks a big job into more manageable pieces. For every season, there is an organizational job to be done.

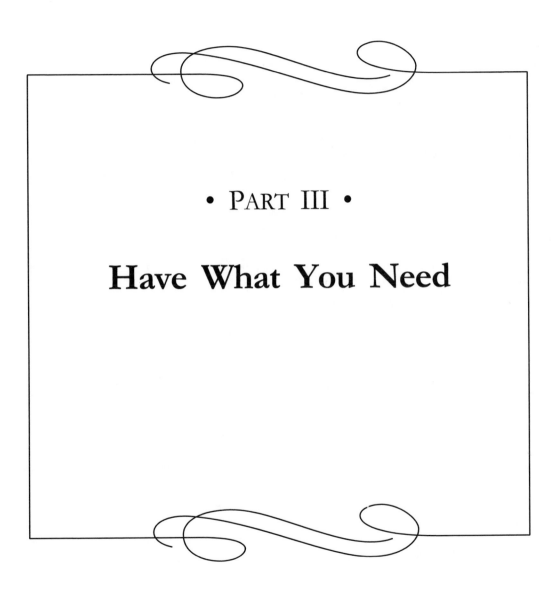

• PART III •

Have What You Need

• 11 •
Setting Up Efficient Workspaces

You may give little thought to your workspaces at home. Things that you would never do on the job, you often routinely do at home, such as trying to work with broken or inadequate equipment or while standing in a mess. Thinking about your home workspaces in a new way involves a cognitive shift. But by making this change, you respect the time and life energy that you are putting into your work at home.

Efficient home workspaces will make it faster and easier for you to work. They will encourage others to work too. The two spaces you should pay particular attention to are the kitchen and the laundry area because of the amount of time you spend there. But the principles apply to any area of your home. By thinking through the kind of work that takes place there, you can make these spaces more suited to your needs.

Eliminate Clutter from Your Work Area

It's hard to work with clutter. The kitchen, for example, is often a place that gets really "decorated" with odds and ends and knickknacks. Resist this temptation. Try to keep your counters as clear as you can (less stuff to clean). Also, be judicious about decorations that you put up on the wall or on top of the counters. While you want your kitchen to be pleasant, it also has to work. The kitchen and bath have lots of moist heat that combines with dust to make guck. Everything in these rooms should be very cleanable.

If you have a laundry area in your home, make sure that it is clutter-free, too. The laundry area often becomes the depository of loose change, missing socks, odds and ends of clothing, and pocket contents. Have handy a trash can and a bin for transporting loose articles to other places in your home. Also, try to arrange this space so you have somewhere to fold clothes. It can be a challenge to fit a folding area in or near this space, but if you can, it will make laundry much easier for you. Even if you do laundry away from home, you need a place to sort, fold, or mend at home.

Have What You Need

It's easy to procrastinate, or *never* do something, if you have to go to another room to get what you need. Think about the supplies and tools you need in each area, and make sure that they are within reach.

Think about Your Physical Comfort

In thinking about your workspaces, ask yourself the following questions.

- Is there enough light?

- Is the area too hot or cold?

- Is there a comfortable place to sit or stand?

- Is it a pleasant place to be?

If you answered "no" to any of these questions, try to think about what you could do to make things more comfortable for yourself.

In subsequent chapters, I describe in more detail what you need to have in each room. But for now, I want to get you used to thinking about the importance of your workspace and how it influences the quality of—and even your willingness to do—your daily work at home.

• 12 •
The Soap Opera

Cleansers are a significant source of clutter and expense and can expose you to some highly toxic chemicals. Knowing about soap can help reduce all three.

The Glory of General-Purpose Cleansers

For most of your cleaning, a neutral, general-purpose cleaner will do the trick. Some examples include concentrates such as Simple Green, dish soap, and liquid hand soap. A general-purpose cleanser will even do windows. (Mix a squirt or two of liquid hand or dish soap into a small bowl of water. Wet your windows or mirrors with this solution with a rag and run a squeegee over them. You'll get great nontoxic results.) Neutral cleaner in a squirt bottle also works well on counters, floors, and cabinets. For a greasy mess, try applying a squirt or two of straight dish soap before adding water. It will break up the grease more easily than if it is diluted.

Specialized Cleansers

If you want to add a few more specialized cleaners to your arsenal, add glass cleaner and a disinfectant for the bathroom. Health experts warn not to use antibacterial products in the kitchen for fear of creating "super bugs," and because you don't want these products around food. For more heavy-duty action, products made of orange oil are very good (like Goo Gone, Orange Clean, DesolvIt). They are especially good at removing grime from plastic surfaces. (I haven't had as much luck with insecticides made of orange oil, but they make the ants smell nice.)

The Well-Ordered Home

Reducing Toxicity

There are a number of nontoxic, "yuppie" cleansers on the market. These are nice, but they can be very expensive. By doing most of your cleaning with neutral and orange-based cleaners, you will have already reduced chemical toxicity. I would avoid anything with ingredients ending in the letters "ene" (like "xylene"). Also, bleach is handy for certain types of cleaning but can be very toxic to breathe. Use sparingly. A dropper or two of 100 percent tea-tree oil in a squirt bottle of water is a good nontoxic antifungal, and can be used in fabric. For those occasions when you do need to use a stronger cleanser. Pouring is often preferable. Using aerosal and spray bottles (in that order) are more likely to lead to your inhaling their contents. Be sure that the area is well ventilated, and keep *all* cleaning products away from children.

Less Is More

Often we think that neutral cleansers do not work because they leave streaks behind. The problem might be that you are mixing them too strongly. There are a couple of possible solutions. First, you can measure the amount of soap you put in, purchase premeasured packets that you add to water, or use "metered" bottles, which have a small compartment on top that you add concentrate to. These automatically tell you the right amount. (Packets, squirt bottles, and metered bottles are available at Don Aslett's Clean Report. www.cleanreport.com.)

Knowing about soap can save time, money, and your lungs. You'll also buy fewer cleaning products, and the area under your sink will look a lot less cluttered.

• 13 •
Ode to Cleaning Supplies

In the previous chapter, you found out lots more than you probably wanted to know about soap. In this chapter, I describe soap's companions—the humble cleaning supply. Make sure that you're fully stocked not only in soap, but in stuff to go with it.

Cleaning Towels

Keep a good assortment of 100 percent cotton towels and rags; 100 percent cotton is important because they will not be absorbent otherwise. These can be pricey, but a good alternative is to buy white cotton terry towels or bar wipes at the local restaurant supply or warehouse discount store. They're great and reasonably priced.

The Hierarchy of Rags

In your kitchen, you need towels that are in good shape. This is more psychological than anything else. Dirty-looking rags around food aren't very appealing, even if they're actually clean. When towels start to get threadbare, faded, or stained, retire them to your "rag" pile. These can be a good substitute for paper towels. When they are really bad, put them out in the garage to use on projects like paint cleanup and furniture refinishing.

Another suggestion is to keep a small plastic hamper in your kitchen for your kitchen towels and rags. It should be plastic since it will be holding wet things. Hang them on the side to dry before putting them in the basket, or they'll be in really bad shape before you have a chance to wash them.

Squirt Bottles

One simple item that can save you loads of money is a set of squirt bottles. You can get these at warehouse clubs and janitor supply stores, and they allow you to mix up your own cleansers for a very reasonable price. You can either use concentrate from a gallon jug (be sure to measure), or premeasured packets (these are available from the Clean Report—www.cleanreport.com).

Lambs' Wool Dusters

These are great for basic dusting and can make things look nice in a hurry. Wal-Mart is an inexpensive source for these, but they are also available at stores that carry kitchen- and housewares.

Scrubbers

I'm not a huge fan of sponges since they can get pretty rank. But I do love 3M Scotch Brite scrubbing pads. These don't rust, can be washed, and are gentle for many surfaces (don't use on plastic). And when they need to be retired, they work great for refinishing furniture. You should also have a selection of scrub brushes: one for your fingernails, old toothbrushes for detailing and getting into tight spaces, and some bigger ones for big jobs.

Squeegees

I can't leave this chapter without mentioning one of my favorite tools—the common squeegee. These produce such superior results on mirrors and windows that you will immediately abandon all efforts to clean windows with other items.

Good cleaning supplies will repay you many times over. And while cleaning may still take work, using good supplies makes sure that your time is used wisely and well.

• 14 •
The Workable Laundry Area

Laundry is one of those tasks that we all have to do, and I don't think anyone particularly likes it. Yet, if we let it go too long, it can really pile up. With some forethought and organization, you can make this task more pleasant.

Have What You Need

There are some specific items that will make your time in the laundry area more efficient. If you don't have a washer and dryer at home, set up these supplies where you are likely to be folding and sorting your laundry.

Stain stick. Shout and Spray and Wash both make solid sticks for stains that are very effective. Keep one near your laundry baskets and get everyone in the habit of using it before they put dirty clothes in the hamper.

Other stain removers. Keep an enzyme presoak, such as Biz, handy for biologic stains (like blood), and Goo Gone for sticky or greasy stains. Goo Gone is the only thing I've ever found that will remove grease from cotton knit.

Mending supplies. Over the long haul, you can save quite a bit of money by doing simple mending yourself. This means sewing on buttons, repairing small tears, and fixing hems that are starting to come out. Some supplies to keep on hand include thread (a set of small multicolored spools of thread costs one to three dollars), a pin cushion, needles, beeswax (to keep thread from becoming knotted), scissors, and a darning egg. (These are hard to find new since no one darns socks anymore. But they are very handy for repairing small holes in knits, such as T-shirts. Look for them in sewing stores.) You can store the extra buttons you get with your clothes here, too. I generally keep needles threaded with white and black thread so that repairs are quick and easy to do.

Garment groomer. This is another handy item to have that can keep your clothes looking good for many years. It is a little shaver that takes "pills" off of fabrics. These typically run about three dollars, and are worth every cent.

Handwashing supplies. Your need for these may depend on the type of clothing you have, but handwashing often is more convenient than taking stuff to the dry cleaners.

Iron and ironing board. As much as most people hate to iron, occasionally we have something that needs it. It's good to have this handy to your laundry area as well. That way, you are more likely to take care of it in small batches rather than waiting until you have nothing to wear. A squirt bottle with plain water can be helpful both for ironing and sometimes as a substitute for ironing if something is lightly wrinkled. Squirt the item with water and let it dry. This works great for travel, too.

Lint roller. I finally broke down and bought one of these, and it's great. If you have pets, this item is a must.

A well-stocked laundry area can save hundreds of dollars by keeping your clothing in good repair. Once you have your supplies at hand, it will be so quick and easy, you'll wish you had done it sooner.

• 15 •
The Essential Kitchen:
Have What You Need to Cook

Many of our kitchens seem to be simultaneously loaded with stuff we don't need and spectacularly lacking in what we do need. As with any high-use area, give some serious thought to making sure that you have what you need. It's helpful to think about tools by task.

Food Prep

For starters, have at least two cutting boards. If you are cutting raw meat, you'll not want to use it for anything else. Your other cutting board can be used for produce, cheese, or anything else (nonmeat) that you need to cut during meal preparation.

Next, take a look at your knives. Most people have way too many, and almost none of them are sharp. This is silly and dangerous. It's quite easy to have an accident with a dull knife (which is often sharp enough to cut you). Get your good knives sharpened, and get rid of any that cannot be. You probably need fewer than you have. I suggest, at a minimum, a paring knife, a chef's knife, and a knife with a serrated edge. These will handle most tasks. And while we're on this subject, I want to mention knife storage. It's important for you to store them safely, either in a rack that fits in a drawer, on a magnetic strip, or in a block. If the knives touch each other, their blades can become dull or even be ruined. You also need to consider safe storage if children live in your home or visit frequently.

A couple of other things that you'll need are a sharp vegetable peeler, a pair of kitchen scissors, a nonelectric can opener, at least one colander, mixing bowls, and a grater. If you eat a lot of lettuce (not counting the bag o' salad kind), a salad spinner can be very handy, too. All of these items should be stored in active storage, preferably near your food-prep area.

Cooking

For cooking basics, I recommend at least a three- and a four-quart saucepan with lids, a small stockpot, and a wok or saute pan. You can add lots of things to these basics, but these will get you started. You'll also need long-handled spoons in both stainless steel and nylon (for coated surfaces), spatulas, and whisks. Get a good set of measuring cups and spoons. Near your stove, you need several good-sized pot holders. Wash these regularly, and retire them when they get ratty.

For baking, you'll need a nine by thirteen-inch pan, a nine by nine-inch pan, a pie pan, at least two cookie sheets, and at least one cooling rack. With these you can cook almost anything in your oven. Keep these near your stove.

Cleaning Up

For food storage, you'll need several decent plastic food containers in assorted sizes with lids. If you have a mismatched set (like most people), line them all up and get rid of containers with no lids, lids with no containers, and anything that is partially melted or badly stained. Replace as necessary. Keep these handy, and you'll really save you in how much you use plastic wrap and other disposable items. Don't microwave in them, however, because it ruins them, and more importantly, because they release plastic particles into your food. Use glass instead for microwaving, even if your container is microwave safe. Remember, "microwave safe" means safe for the dish, not necessarily for you.

After you have these basic items, you can add whatever you want. But with these items, you'll be able to perform most tasks you need. Everything else is gravy (gravy boat optional).

• 16 •
The Well-Stocked Pantry

Pantries have fallen out of favor in recent years. But they are a key component of household organization. While we often buy too much refrigerated and perishable food (see chapter 37), we don't buy enough of other types of food and necessities. We rely on an infrastructure of interstate shipping to keep goods available. But one good snowstorm can show you how flimsy this system is when grocery shelves get wiped out. A well-stocked pantry gives you a buffer. You can dip into to it for easy meals. It also provides a cushion for you and your family in the event of illness, natural disaster, or a loss of electrical power. Keep a stash of food and toiletry items on hand at all times.

Creating Your Pantry

You can create a pantry anywhere. It doesn't even need to be located in the kitchen (although that's the most convenient place for it). You can stash food items anywhere that you have room, as long as you keep track of where they are. This can include your garage, basement, or even under a bed. A pantry can have provisions for anywhere from a few days to a few months. As an initial goal, you might aim to have enough supplies on hand to last you and your family for a period of one week.

What Goes into a Pantry?

That's really up to you. I recommend that you stock it with items that you generally use. If you like canned soups, buy those. If you enjoy tuna, buy that. Dried cereal, baking goods (like sugar or flour), pasta, and canned beans and meats are pantry staples. You might also keep a stash of jarred spaghetti sauce.

Some people include a well-stocked freezer as part of their pantries. That's okay as long as you regularly rotate items instead of having them becoming part of the frozen wasteland. The point is to start where you are. Know what you and your family particularly enjoy, and buy accordingly. To begin, buy two or three of the items that you normally purchase only one of. Store them together. As you finish an item, add it to your shopping list, and remember to put the new items to the back and use the older items first.

For certain items such as flour and sugar, you may want to repackage them in plastic or glass to keep the bugs out. If you are using a single storage area, group similar items together (like soups, canned beans, jars of spaghetti sauce). Another option is to group items by meal type. Breakfast items together, spaghetti sauce and pasta together, soup and crackers together). That way, it is easy for anyone in the household to put together a meal.

You too can have the secret weapon of an organized home. Here are some ideas to get you started.

- Pick a place. This can be even a shelf or part of a cupboard.

- Start stocking up. List or keep in mind items you use all the time.

- Start keeping multiple numbers of these items, and work from there.

- Keep an inventory listing. As your pantry grows, begin to keep a written inventory. This can also serve as a grocery list. Print out multiple copies and keep them on the inside of the cupboard door. As you run out of certain items, note them on your inventory list. (Sample inventory lists are available at www.organizedhome.com.)

Try starting a small pantry after your next trip to the store, and see if meal prep and planning gets a little bit easier.

• 17 •
Five Things You Should Never Run Out Of

There are going to be times when you miscalculate and run out of something you need. But there are some things that you should to never run out of. These items often have no substitute. And if you are low at a crucial time, such as the middle of the night, being out of something you need can create a unnecessary crisis—or at the very least, make things quite inconvenient. With a little planning, you can make sure this doesn't happen to you.

Toilet Paper

There is no reason to run out of this. I'm always amazed when people buy this in a four pack. Why would you do that? Unless you live alone, never have any company, or have absolutely no storage space, it makes sense to buy this item in bulk. The times that you're using a lot (like when you have some horrible stomach flu) are hardly the times when you feel like shopping. And there aren't a lot of ready substitutes, unless you count tissues. But lets face it—if you're out of TP, what are the chances that you have tissues? Membership warehouse stores and even many large grocers sell this by the twenty pack. Stock up, and don't let your stash get below four rolls.

Gasoline

If you have a car, keep it gassed and ready to go. There is never a good time to run out of gas, and it could be really bad in case of an emergency. When you hit the half-tank mark, go fill up. By using this as a mark, you can also gas up at a cheaper station instead of whatever is at hand. This saves both aggravation and money.

Prescription Medications

If you're on maintenance medication for a chronic condition, don't run out of it! Many of these drugs are only effective when there is a steady level in your bloodstream. You can't achieve that if you haven't taken your meds for days because you've run out. In some cases, the results can be life threatening. And many prescriptions, such as for pain medications, cannot be renewed over the phone. If possible, take advantage of your pharmacy's program to mail prescription medications to you at certain intervals, or note on your calendar when you will need to get a refill.

Film

As picture taking moves into the digital age, this suggestion may soon become obsolete. But until it is, make it a point to keep at least one roll of film on hand. We often miss wonderful moments because our cameras are empty. Whenever you take a roll of film in for developing (or mail it in), buy a replacement. Better yet, stock up so that you're always ready to capture life's remarkable moments.

Pet Supplies

Animals are great, but they are also a responsibility. They depend on you to take care of them. Don't run out of food, litter, or other supplies, unless you like making last-minute trips out. There really aren't many substitutes for cat food (dogs will eat anything) or cat litter. Food for smaller animals, birds, and fish is also a challenge. These animals are depending on you to meet their needs. When you start to get low, stock up the next time you're out.

• 18 •

Avoiding the Vacation from Hell Begins at Home

We all have stories about some horrid vacation we've taken. This is unfortunate. Vacations should be a time of rest and renewal. But often, they're just the opposite. Some problems with travel are inevitable. But you can avoid many of them with a little planning and foresight.

Plan Trips Closer to Home

We often feel that we must travel a long way to have a vacation. Not true! Explore some of the areas in your own backyard. It will probably be cheaper and will result in less wear and tear on you.

Start Preparing Two Weeks before Departure

Last minute preparations for a trip tend to be highly stressful. In the week or two before you leave, start gathering what you need in a "staging area." Consider developing a packing list. You can refine it as you go, and then you'll have it for next time.

Take a Trip That You Can Afford

Travel within your means. Spending more than you can afford can make everyone cranky and tense. Sadly, I see many families behaving badly on vacation, and I believe that some of the tension is due to how much they're spending.

Security Planning

Before you go, pull any credit cards that you won't need or other superfluous stuff out of your purse. Photocopy your credit cards (front and back), identification (license and passport), and any other information you would need in case you lose your purse. Keep one copy in your suitcase and another with a trusted friend at home (preferably one with access to a fax machine). If you are traveling with a laptop or PDA, back up everything before you leave, and leave the backup copy at home. Record the serial number of your laptop somewhere at home too.

Plan for Delays and Canceled Flights

In the wake of September 11, the landscape of our airports has changed forever. Increased security means longer lines. And even before that tragedy, delays were already a fact of life when flying. While you can't change that your trip may be delayed by security or the weather, advance planning can make all the difference in your comfort. This is especially critical if you are flying with children.

Always pack food and water when flying. Even for a short flight, you could be delayed and forced to sit on the tarmac for hours with no food and water. This makes everyone ugly! If you are traveling with a baby who drinks formula, pack more than you think you'll need. There are no substitutes for this on an airplane.

Pack an emergency kit. I always pack an emergency kit in my carry-on bag. In my emergency kit, I pack my prescription medications (always have these in both your suitcase and your carry-on bag), clean underwear, toothpaste, a toothbrush, and a small container of shampoo. That way, if my bag gets lost (as happened recently on a trip to Washington, DC), I can still feel like a human being.

Dress comfortably. Be sure to always dress comfortably when you fly. Wear something that would be presentable if your suitcase got lost, but that you can sit in for a long time. You'll be happier, and you'll be able to move quickly in case of an emergency.

Travel can be a richly rewarding activity. And while you can't plan for every contingency, some advance preparation will help you avoid the vacation from hell.

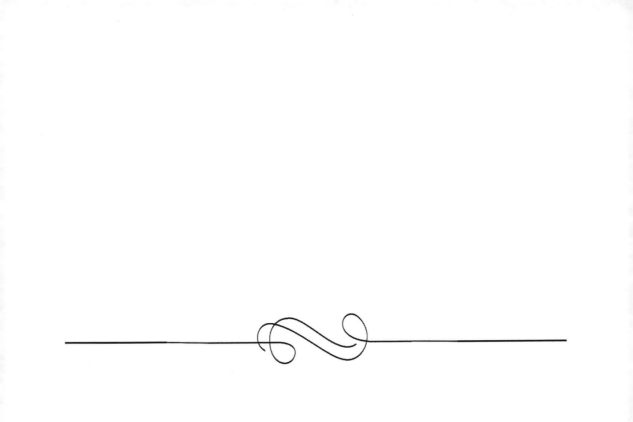

• 19 •
Order to Go

I recently saw a movie where the highly organized heroine opened her jacket to reveal an emergency kit strapped to her waist. Everything was right at her fingertips. I was jealous and wanted one! And the good news is, we can. Here are some suggestions for having what we need—to go.

The Organized Purse

Women carry around a lot of junk and often end up with a purse the size of a battleship. We tend to think of purses as fashion accessories and not tools. But they can be both. Choose your purse wisely. Buy one with built-in compartments and organizers so that you can find things easily.

Have What You Need

I encourage you to carry around only what you need and trim the excess. Basics are your credit cards (but not all of them), ATM card, identification, AAA card, health-insurance card, and any other cards that you use on a regular basis or need in an emergency. Leave the rest at home. (Photocopy the fronts and backs of any cards you carry and keep this list at home. In the event of theft, you will have the numbers to call.) You will need a checkbook (or at least one check), a place for keys, sunglasses, and cash. Regularly pull change from you purse when it starts getting too heavy. Here are some other things to consider carrying. I have these in several small kits in my purse.

Kit 1. Mending kit, Band-Aids (several sizes), small packets of ibuprofen or Tylenol (you can get these from Viking Office Supplies), Shout wipes (for stains), wet wipes (for general cleanup), and safety pins.

Kit 2. Mini, portable office with Post-its, data flags, paper clips, binder clips, and rubber bands.

Kit 3. Swiss Army knife (with scissors), mini flashlight, mini mirror, comb, eyeglass repair kit. (Be sure to remove the Swiss Army knife from your purse before traveling by air.)

Portable Office

This is handy when you travel or work away from your desk, and is the expanded version of the one I carry in my purse. Start by getting a small plastic cosmetic bag. I prefer clear plastic so I can see everything. Buy mini scissors (not the ones with the plastic blades), tape, a glue stick, correction tape or fluid, paper clips, Post-its, binder clips, rubber bands, address and return-address labels, mini stapler, marker, pen, highlighter, stamps, and a small notepad.

Safe Car

Even with careful planning, things can still happen to your car. It's important to take at least some minimal precautions to ensure your safety if you break down. Assemble an auto-safety kit for each car.

Flares (so people can see you if you are broken down by the side of the road), a "Help" sign, jumper cables, a tire inflator, an emergency blanket and hand/foot warmers (important in cold climates—look in camping supplies), bottled water (especially in hot climates), a cell phone, a rain poncho, and a hammer for breaking windows. I also keep insect repellant, flying insect spray (for wasps and yellow jackets that fly in), and sun block in both of our cars.

Order to go will make you more prepared than a Boy Scout. If you're going to lug stuff around, make sure it's useful. And maybe they'll make a movie about you.

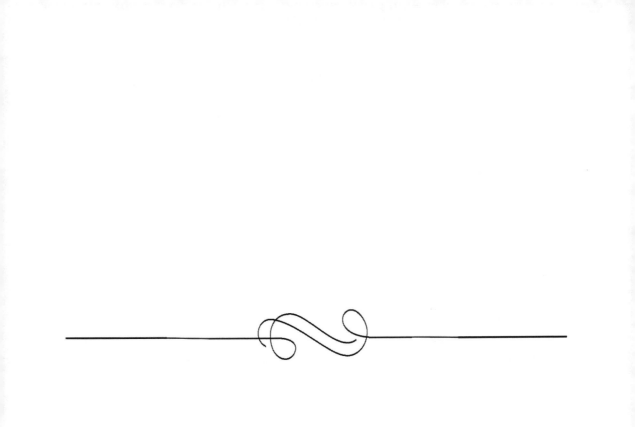

• 20 •

Organized Entertaining:
Making It Fun to Have People Over

I used to dread having people over, even though most of the reasons were in my own mind. I thought that my apartment or house had to be perfect. I made way too big a deal about what I would serve. It became a four-day ordeal to get ready. And my guests, not realizing that I had been preparing for days, didn't seem nearly appreciative enough.

My first inkling that organization could improve this situation was after I had done my first round of major dejunking. Some relatives were coming to visit, and it only took an hour to get the house ready. When they arrived, they commented on how nice and clean everything looked, and we had a great visit. Another turning point was when I joined a church that had weekly meetings in different church members' homes. Suddenly, I was having company on a regular basis. It was simplify—or else. Through these experiences, I learned that organization makes it easier to have people over. Let me show you what I mean.

General Organization Makes for Easy Party Prep

If you have dejunked and have your cleaning supplies handy, it will take you much less time to prep your house. In fact, it probably won't need much prep because it's already in good shape.

Have Some Supplies Always on Hand

Keep a stash of paper plates and napkins, plastic forks, and other supplies handy at all times. If you have a large group, this is the way to go. But even for a smaller gathering, having the option of disposable items can make things easier. (Avoid Styrofoam, if at all possible, since it's very hard on the environment.) I always keep birthday candles on hand, too. This makes last-minute birthday celebrations much easier to pull off.

Simplify Preparations

Sometimes entertaining is not fun because we have unrealistic expectations about what we need to do. The watchword is "simplify."

Simplify food. You don't need to cook for days or prepare meals that are complex. Unless you love to cook, elaborate preparations can suck all the fun out of entertaining in a hurry. Instead, opt for foods that are easy to prepare. Your guests are coming to see *you,* not your food. Barbequed chicken, fresh corn, and watermelon make a great dinner. In winter, a roasted chicken with baked potatoes, steamed vegetables, and a salad is also easy to prepare.

Simplify cleaning. Be realistic about the cleanliness of your home, too. It really doesn't have to be perfect, as long as it's tidy. Again, your guests are coming to see you, not your home. And if someone is coming who is likely to perform a "white-glove test," it will probably be less stressful to meet them someplace else. (Of course, some of these folks are relatives, and moving the meeting is often easier said than done.) As you start making conscious lifestyle choices (for example, giving up the belief that you must be perfect), you'll be buffered from critical remarks, too.

Having people over needn't be an ordeal. As it gets easier for you to entertain, you'll start inviting more people into your life. And this may become one of the most positive changes that you make.

• 21 •
Creating a Gift Cupboard

Want to save some serious money? Start a gift cupboard. The basic strategy is to anticipate your needs and take advantage of sales and markdowns. Let me show you how it works.

Anticipate Your Needs

Start by thinking about your gift-giving needs for the upcoming year. For example, are there children you routinely buy for, either at Christmas or for birthdays? Are there relatives that you send gifts to? Who is on your regular shopping list for Christmas or Hanukkah? Are there any graduations coming up? Any babies due? Any people getting married? Do you need to buy any teacher gifts? Once you have this list, either on paper or in your head, you're ready to begin.

Watch for Sales

The next thing to do is to keep your eyes open. Stores often have sales, particularly during changes in season. The markdowns during these times of the year can be from 30 percent to 50 percent of their normal price.

Of course, the best sales take place at the end of the year. Some of you already know this since you stock up on gift wrap and cards at half price. But even more bargains await. This is where the discipline comes in, because the last thing you feel like doing at the end of the year is more shopping! But if you keep your eyes open, you can buy things for anywhere between 50 percent and 80 percent off of the normal price. The best prices are for toys, winter clothing, and Christmas decorations, because stores want to get rid of them. But next winter, they will be loved and appreciated—and you won't be paying full price. Toys are great to stock up on if you have children that you routinely buy for.

Find a Storage Place

You will also need a place to store the items you purchase. If at all possible, store these together so that you'll know where to look when it is time to give them away. If you can't store gifts together, note where they are on your calendar near the dates you need them. Throughout the year, you'll find other items on sale. Keep your gift list in mind, and pick up gifts as you see them. You may need to fill in with nonsale items, but these will be far fewer than if you wait to buy a gift when you need it.

Gift Wrapping: Have What You Need

You will also want to keep a good supply of gift wrapping on hand. I keep all-occasion wrap, birthday, wedding, and baby wrap, gift bags, cards, ribbons, and marking pens on hand. I usually stock up on these at paper outlet stores or discounters. I've also found that cellophane wrap can help make a wonderful gift basket, and can turn an ordinary plate of cookies into something special. Following the principle of active storage, I keep my Christmas wrap separate, only pulling it out close to the holidays.

As the holidays approach, I dig through my stash of gifts and start making piles for various households. I then put each of the family piles in separate boxes, and one by one wrap the gifts in each box. Then I note which people still don't have a gift and buy accordingly. Before I know it, my Christmas gifts are done.

Try stocking a gift cupboard. You won't regret it.

• 22 •
Don't Kill a Fly with a Baseball Bat

I love gadgets. I've always had an appreciation for things that work well, make me more efficient, and allow me to do things I wouldn't ordinarily do. I love electronic devices, too, and I know I'm not alone. Some are truly nifty. Others seem pretty ridiculous (electric nose-hair clippers spring to mind).

However, as exciting as new tools are, they are often expensive. The newer and more novel an item, the more you're going to pay. Also, today's cool gadgets can be tomorrow's source of clutter and junk. The trick is to learn to separate the useful from the junk. To do that, we must get into the habit of constantly asking ourselves whether another gadget is really necessary.

As an example, let's take personal digital assistants (PDAs) versus a paper date book. Is electronic always better? That depends. Earlier this month, I was chatting with an elderly woman at an office-supply store. I was helping her dig through the pile of personal organizers that were on sale. In weighing the pros and cons of the various date books and organizers, I asked if she had ever considered getting an electronic organizer. Apparently, her children had been after her to "go digital" too, and she was having none of it. She pointedly told me that she was too old to learn how to use a computer, that she saw no need for one, and that she had no interest. At that point, I held up my hands and drew her attention back to the pile of date books. Clearly, an electronic organizer would not be a good choice for her.

I didn't buy one either for quite some time. I could get around quite well with a paper date book, and there didn't seem to be any advantage to the other approach. It wasn't until I was at a meeting and observed a colleague with all her important information handy in her PDA that I began to consider it. A paper version of this information would be inches thick and could not be easily slipped into a purse or pocket. Suddenly, it *did* make sense for me to have one. I got one a few weeks after that, and I use it all the time.

When considering purchasing a new item, ask yourself the following.

- What will this item help me do?

- Do I *need* to do that task?

- Can I do it with what I already have?

- Will the item make me more efficient than what I already have?

- Does the change in efficiency justify the cost?

My point is not for you to avoid all technology, devices, or products that promise to ease some aspect of your life. But don't assume that *buying* something is always the answer. We can clear out many cleaning products when we realize that soap and water can do quite a lot. But there is room for a few specialized products. A new computer program *can* make you more efficient, but only if the task that it performs is something you actually need to do. A handy kitchen gadget might be really helpful, or it can become next spring's yard sale item. As you become more knowledgeable about how you work, and what type of work you are most likely to do, you'll become more savvy about which items help, and which are clutter. In short, you'll stop trying to kill a fly with a baseball bat when a flyswatter will work just as well.

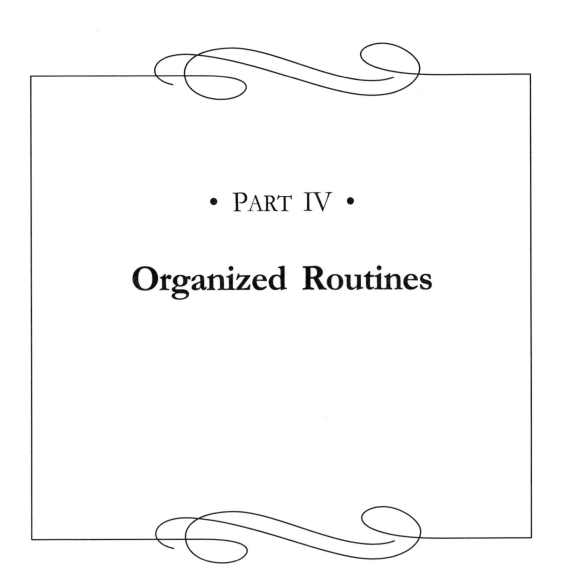

• PART IV •

Organized Routines

• 23 •
Can You Find Your Stuff?

It happens every day. A home looks neat on the surface (music swells). But true horror lurks just beneath the surface, ready to pounce on some unsuspecting soul. And then, someone opens a drawer or closet—aaaahhhhh (piercing scream)!

Messy closets and drawers are common, even in generally neat homes. They are also a symptom of a basic misunderstanding about storage: putting things away is only one half of storage. Retrieval is the other half. Next time you're tempted to just shove something in a drawer, stop and think about finding it again. Here are some strategies to help you think about storage *and* retrieval.

Think Function

One approach is to think about the function of the item. Where are you more likely to use something? Store it as close to where you use it as possible. For example, this means storing your extra toilet paper under the sink in all your bathrooms. I would even keep a roll or two in a basket on the back of the toilet (you'll be glad later). Keep items that go on the table (like tablecloths, placemats, and trivets) near the table. Keep dishes near the dishwasher or kitchen sink. As you start thinking about the function of items, you will develop a workable storage plan.

Put Similar Items Together

Another strategy is to keep similar items together. Some categories may include all gift items that you buy ahead, painting equipment, or yard tools. Knowing that you now keep all gifts you buy in your basement cupboard will make it easier to find them when you need them. As you locate items around the house or buy new ones that fit into each category, take them to their designated place and you'll be able to find them again.

Use Memory Cues

When you're searching for something six months from now, what cue will help you remember where to look? You might need to jot yourself a note in your calendar to help you locate something. Try to make memory connections with anything that you put away. Storing by function or with similar items together can also provide memory cues.

Getting Started

You might start by emptying one cupboard or shelf and beginning to sort. As you find stuff that belongs in another spot, put it there (or near that spot, if the space is crowded). Keep working on the original cupboard until you are finished. Then move on to the next one.

As you sort, you will find things you thought were gone for good or that you even forgot you had. You'll use more of what you already own, and it will feel like you've been on a giant shopping spree—without spending a dime. Once you get a handle on your storage woes, you'll have to periodically sort through your cupboards, drawers, and storage areas to nab anything that's not in an appropriate place. But having a designated storage area will make it much more likely that you'll put stuff away and will make it a snap for you to find it again.

• 24 •
Alphabetizing: It's Not Just for Obsessive-Compulsives

I vividly remember the first time I saw something alphabetized in a home. I was at the home of a colleague, and noticed that his record albums were all alphabetized. I promptly made fun of him. In the years since, I've come to realize that he was right. (But of course, I'll never admit it to him.) Alphabetizing is a strategy that can save you time and frustration when you're trying to find things. So what are good things to alphabetize? Alphabetize anything you have a lot of, and from which you sometimes need to draw specific items. Here are some good candidates.

Videos and DVDs

Most people have a sizeable collection of videos and DVDs. Before alphabetizing, sort them by type. For example, exercise videos and instructional videos can be separated from movies. Children's videos can also be separated. While you are sorting through your collection, pull any that your family has outgrown or that you never liked. Donate these (libraries will often take them) or find a family with children younger than yours that may like them. Once you have sorted them by type, alphabetize them by the name of the movie. If you are storing them in boxes, label the outside to know what the range is (for instance, "A-F"). You'll be able to locate the video you want within seconds.

CDs

The average family now has anywhere from two hundred to eight hundred (or even one thousand) CDs. You need to have a system or you'll never end up with the CD that you want. First, sort all your CDs by type. You may consider pulling your children's CDs and storing them separately. Use broad categories (like classical, rock, pop, folk, gospel, or movie soundtracks). Within those categories, alphabetize by the name of the artist, group, or composer. For example, for classical music, I would generally alphabetize by composer. However, if there is a particular artist (say, Sarah Brightman), I would alphabetize by her last name. Also, if there is a collection with selections from more than one artist, I alphabetize that by the name of the CD itself. Do this within each category, and you'll be able to find what you want immediately.

Spices

This last suggestion will convince your friends that you're nuts, but stick with me on this. Yes, I'm suggesting that you alphabetize your spices. Spices are something else that you tend to have a lot of and that you need to get specific items from. Alphabetizing helps you find what you need and also shows you immediately when you have bought too much of any one spice. For this task, I recommend that you get a spice rack where you can see everything at once. (I'm not crazy about lazy Susans because stuff tends to get buried.) Once you have your rack in place, pull out everything and put it in alphabetical order. Alphabetize by the name of the spice, not any adjectives that describe it (for instance, ground pepper, red pepper, and black pepper are all filed under "P"). Make sure you can read the label without having to remove the jar from the rack.

I'm convinced that once you try alphabetizing, you'll like it so much that you won't care what your friends think. In fact, you may persuade them to join you!

• 25 •
Dare to Be a Label Queen

Fair warning. Labeling things is bound to get *you* labeled. But this strategy will save you so much aggravation that the teasing will be well worth it. Again, the main thing you're trying to accomplish is to minimize time spent thrashing around. If you have things labeled, you can reach in and grab what you need without having to pull out each and every similar item.

Some Good Candidates for Labeling

If you can't tell what something is at a glance, it deserves a label. For example, my husband is a computer programmer. He has about thirty CDs that he must use on a regular basis. They were neatly placed in a rack, but had no labels on the ends. So one night, I took apart the CD cases and labeled the ends. Now every time my husband needs one of these, he can pull it out in seconds instead of having to pull out every single one. Labels save him several minutes each time he searches, and those minutes can really add up over the course of a day.

Labels for Containers, Drawers, and Shelves

Other candidates for labels are containers, or even drawers whose contents tend to be somewhat mysterious to you. You can label shelves. This can be handy when you have other people putting stuff away. I have two built-in pumps for soap at my kitchen sink. *I* know which one is dish soap and which one is hand soap. But now I've labeled them so that other people do, too.

Labeling in Kitchen and Office

Similarly, I labeled my containers in the pantry so that I can tell at a glance which one is flour and which one is powered sugar (this is preferable to pulling them out and tasting them each time). I also label the jar lids of my spices, since that is the end that shows in my rack. I label my files. I label boxes of storage stuff in my closet, spines of notebooks in my office, and travel bottles filled with shampoo, conditioner, and sunscreen.

A Helpful Gadget

Most of the suggestions in this book can be done very inexpensively, but now I'm going to suggest one somewhat pricey gadget—a label maker. These range from twenty to eighty dollars at office-supply stores. I like the P-touch by Brother. Now why would I suggest this if you can just write labels by hand? Yes, hand labeling is cheap and doesn't require a gadget. But the results of the P-touch are so spectacular that you will never turn back. It gives you a variety of sizes, too. I use it to label Pendaflex folders, CDs, everything in my kitchen—you name it. As for the color of your labels, I recommend black print on white or clear tape. I love colors, but these are the easiest to read. Clear is nice if you want to label something like a shelf, and not make it look like your mother packed you for camp.

Labeling will save you time every day. Try it, and you too will be a label queen.

• 26 •
Corral the Mess

"Corralling the mess" refers to those times when you can't put things away right this instant, but need to keep them from spreading throughout the house. Basically, it means keeping a mess within a confined space. Consider this a sanctioned mess.

Let's say, for example, that you don't have time to put your clothes away right now. Corralling the mess means keeping them in a single place in your bedroom, like on a particular chair, so that they're off the floor and not scattered throughout your room. This strategy makes cleanup, when you finally do have some time, much easier to accomplish.

A similar principle can be applied to the kitchen. You may not have time to wash your dishes, but you can scrape and rinse them and stack them neatly by the sink rather than leaving them wherever they happen to land. Corralling the mess can give you a midpoint between just leaving things where they fall and a full cleanup.

Using Containers

You can also corral the mess in places where clutter tends to accumulate. Baskets in key places can make things look tidier. Instead of having a pile of individual items, they can all be in one compact container. To the eye, they look like "one" instead of "many," and that automatically makes things appear less cluttered. Some strategies to help you corral the mess include the following.

- Place baskets or bins in places where clutter accumulates, like the laundry area, bathroom, top of the stairs, and entryway.

- Put a chair or bench in each bedroom.

- Have a basket for toys in every room where children play.

- Have a junk drawer in your kitchen or family room.

Of course, these areas need to be periodically cleaned out. But that can often wait even several weeks. And since the mess is in one concentrated area, it keeps things from being strewn throughout the house.

Living with Others

Corralling the mess is also a strategy that will help you live more peaceably with others, including your partner, roommates, or children. Cleaning and household chores often become a sore point in relationships and can cause a lot of stress. Corralling the mess is one strategy to help you compromise. Basically, the idea is that you let someone be as messy as they want—within a confined space. For example, you may agree to not touch each other's home office. Or you may agree to keep the living room tidy most of the time, but let the family room have a more lived-in look.

This strategy can also work well with small children. Toys tend to migrate. For quick pick-up, have a toy bin or shelf in every room that the kids use. Periodically, you will have to sort through things and match parts that may be scattered across three different rooms. But it will make day-to-day living a little easier and allow you to relax and not feel like everything has to be perfect.

Corralling the mess is a great compromise and can be ideal for busy people. Look around your home, and see if there isn't room for a corral.

• 27 •

Clearing the Way:
Containing Entryway Debris

The entry into your home makes the first impression. But we often give little thought to how this area looks—and worse, to how it functions. When done well, your entryway can corral the clutter that enters your home and contain it. It can also help you remember to bring things you've promised to others and find your keys and purse.

Establish Your Entryway

The first step is to figure out which entry gets used most often. In some cases, that is very easy—there's only one. But in other cases, there may be multiple ways to get into your home. Pick the one that gets used most often.

Set It Up

Once you've established your entryway, set it up to be maximally functional. This may be a small area or a larger entryway or mudroom. In either case, remember that it needs to catch all the stuff you bring in with you.

Key rack. This is a basic. Be sure to have a key rack near your door. Keep only current and functioning keys on it, and have enough hooks for everyone in the family with keys.

Coat and purse rack. Another basic. Have a place to take off your coat and hang it up. It can be a free-standing rack, a traditional bar with hangers, or shaker pegs. We've replaced bars in our house with Shaker pegs because it's so much easier to hang coats on them (thus making it more likely that people will do it).

A place for umbrellas and such. You'll also want to set up an area for weather implements including umbrellas, hats, scarves, and gloves. Hooks can work well, but if you have a lot of these items, you may want cubbie holes, baskets, or bins. I keep ours in a three-high bin on casters.

School and work supplies. School and work supplies have a way of getting scattered throughout the house. This can lead to a stressful morning routine of trying to find missing homework, books, briefcases, and other items. To catch these items, you might take a lesson from schools and have cubbies or modified lockers (cubbies with hooks underneath). You can purchase these premade, or you can make them yourself. It's helpful for you to have one for each person in your home. That way, books, homework, and anything else that needs to go to school or work the next day can be placed in the cubbie, and it's ready to go.

A place for outgoing. You might also have items you need to take somewhere on a regular basis. This kind of stuff usually ends up stacked around so that we remember it. But we often don't. You can solve this problem by designating a place in your entryway for outgoing stuff. I frequently bring stuff with me to church, for example, and have a "church" basket by the door. During the week, I add to this basket as I think of it. Come Sunday morning, I look inside and grab anything I need to take.

The entryway can be a key way of managing the flow in and out of your home. But it can also end up as the junkyard for stuff you can't find a home for. Take a look around as you go about your business, and return things to their proper places. This way, your entryway can look tidy and keep messes corralled, while making it easy to find things on your way out.

• 28 •

Know Where They Are:
The Master Schedule

Activities away from home can dramatically impact your life and the life of your family. If you are responsible for more than yourself, you need a master schedule to keep track of where everyone belongs. Think of yourself as the air-traffic controller for your household.

Decide on a Format

The type of planner you use largely depends on your preferences, the style that works best for you, and how much information you need to keep. For some people or families, a large wall-mounted schedule is the most efficient and easiest way to coordinate activities. For others, a paper date book works. For still others, a Palm Pilot or other type of personal digital assistant (PDA) is the way to go. If in doubt, try a couple and see which one works best for you.

Keep One Master Schedule

You can get into trouble fairly quickly if you record dates and other information in several places at once. Invariably, you'll be looking at the wrong calendar and will double-book something or miss an appointment because it was recorded in the wrong book. Decide which calendar will be the master. Gather all your stray calendars, and transfer all appointment information to your master calendar. Finally, record all new appointments on the master calendar, too. It helps if you can carry it with you at all times.

Coordinate with Family Members

Meet periodically with any family members whose schedules must mesh with yours. Record any upcoming activities on your master calendar. If you have young children, you don't need to "meet" with them, but keep an eye out for papers coming from school or any of their activities. As children mature, start sitting down with them once a week to review any activities that they're planning to do. Be sure to find out about any activities to which you need to contribute (like getting birthday presents or T-shirts for school). This will head off most last-minute surprises. If you are living with or taking care of an elderly relative, any appointments he or she has need to go on your master schedule, too.

Be Proactive with Routine Activities

It's stressful to always be playing catch-up. To get a handle on this, write all activities and deadlines that you know about on your calendar. I have two positions in a volunteer organization. Both require periodic written reports. They don't take long to complete, but the requests for them always seemed to come at the worst times. Now, I have these on my calendar and can plan accordingly.

Even things like haircuts can be planned for. I used to wait until I "needed" a haircut before calling for an appointment. It would generally take two weeks to get in, and by then I would be looking pretty shaggy. Now I just schedule them ahead of time. It's easy. And it's already in my book, so I don't schedule outings at the same time. While you won't be able to anticipate everything, having the routine stuff down will give you a lot more control over your schedule.

Managing your calendar is a major facet of home organization. With some planning and consistent use of your master calendar, you can feel more on top of your schedule and your life.

• 29 •
Rethinking Your Activities

It's a fact of modern life: family members are often like ships passing in the night. Everyone is always rushing from one activity to another. Even toddlers and preschoolers have schedules that are solidly booked. The complication grows by the number of people in your household. Even singles might find that, between work, social life, and other obligations, they're rarely home. Add a spouse and kids to the mix, and is it any wonder that home life—and with it home organization—falls by the wayside?

One source of busyness is children's extracurricular activities. These include sports, clubs, and lessons. As early as 1925, researchers realized that the car was the primary tool by which homemakers accomplished their work. If anything, that is truer today. The U.S. Department of Transportation estimates that a person with children travels forty-nine miles, and makes 4.3 trips *per day.*

People without kids may also find themselves rarely at home. Long commutes, late hours spent working, and involvement in activities can tap into at-home time. While it's great to be out in the world, these activities need to be in balance with the other important tasks in your life.

What Happens When You're Never Home

Being away from home affects home organization on many levels. You're not home, so supplies get depleted and you start running out of things, making the time you do have at home more stressful. The mail and the laundry stack up. Things get messy and lost. There is no time for routine maintenance, so you end up replacing things before their time. In order to get a grip on household organization, you will need to spend at least some time at home. And that involves rethinking each of the activities you and your family get involved in.

Weigh the Costs and Benefits of Each Activity

One key to living a more organized life at home is to be proactive about which activities you and your family participate in. Consider these questions about each activity you are involved in.

- Does it make sense for you or your family to participate?

- Is this a good time to participate?

- Do you or your kids enjoy the activity?

- How much time and money is involved in this activity?

- How does it fit in with other activities and other members of your family?

If you're planning activities for a family, consider what impact each individual activity has on the family as a whole.

If you decide an activity is worthwhile, realize that it's okay to have a busy "season" of your life, as long as you take the time to step back and regroup once that season is over. We tend to get into trouble when we say that life will only be busy for a short time, and then it remains busy after the activity ends. Short spurts are fine. In fact, household organization will make these busy periods easier to manage. But then you need to take a step back, regroup, tidy, restock, and clean up.

Finally, realize that it's okay to say no to even good opportunities. Sometimes it's important to limit your involvement in good and worthwhile activities so that you can be available for the best.

Being selective about activities can give you some much-needed room to breathe. And the happy by-product is that your home will be much easier to manage.

• 30 •
Acknowledging Important Dates

I have to be honest with you. I've never been one of those great folks who manages to always send a card for every birthday, anniversary, or other special occasion. But it's a nice thing to do, so I keep trying. I've also discovered that it's challenging for most people, not just me. There are two main obstacles: knowing (and remembering) the dates and getting the card.

Learning the Dates

Let's address the issue of knowing dates first. Before you start, decide which friends and relatives you are going to acknowledge this way. You need to be somewhat selective, especially if you know a lot of people. For some friends or relatives, you may choose to only acknowledge milestone birthdays (like forty, fifty, and beyond). To find out what you want to know, the most direct way is to simply ask. You can tell folks that you're trying to record everyone's birthdays in a single place, and ask if they could help. (You may need to confess that you've been guessing all these years.) You might also learn of an upcoming important date in casual conversation. If the date is a few weeks off, make note of it in your datebook or PDA. Then, at the very least, you'll remember to say something in person, call, or send an e-mail.

Getting the Cards

It can be a big operation to go to the store, pick the perfect card, write in it, address it, and mail it. It's no wonder that so few people do it. And we're not even talking about the cost of individual cards! These are typically between two and four dollars. Over a year, that can add up to quite a bit of money. So what can you do?

Keep a stash of cards. I'm much more likely to send a note if I have a stash of cards. You can buy a special box for your greeting-card supply. I've found it handy to have Pendaflex folders in my desk drawer with several categories of cards including baby, birthday, get-well-soon, sympathy, congratulations, wedding, anniversary, and thank-you cards. I also keep postcards and blank note cards. I keep these categories stocked by buying in bulk, either from Current, a purveyor of discount cards and gift wrap (www.currentcatalog.com) or from discount stores. For certain special occasions (like Mother's Day), I buy separate cards.

While cards purchased in bulk may not be "perfect," I'm much more likely to actually send one than if I need to make a special trip. Ultimately, the personal note that you write inside is more meaningful than what the greeting card company had to say. And even in bulk, you can buy nice-looking cards.

Don't forget e-mail cards. Or as I like to call them, the procrastinator's friend. These can be sent instantly around the world. While they won't work for everyone on your list, they are a nice alternative to a traditional paper card.

Chuck Perfectionism

As a final word, give yourself permission to not always do this perfectly. There are going to be times when you space out and forget an important date. Life happens. And sometimes it's just not possible for you to get to all the details. The best strategy in this case is to make contact when you do remember. It lets people know that you were thinking of them, and that's what is important. I've never had someone turn down a card (or gift for that matter) simply because it was late.

• 31 •
Some Thoughts on Multitasking

Multitasking is that wonderful ability to perform several tasks at once. Computer moguls may think they invented it, but I know the truth—mothers did. It's a key skill in household and life management. There are examples everywhere—some good, some not so good. Talking on the phone while at the gym. Putting on makeup while driving. While it is an effective technique, like anything, it can be overdone. In this chapter, I review two types of multitasking and describe their limitations.

Have Several Projects Going at Once

Devout multitaskers know this technique well; in any busy home or work environment, it's an important skill. Basically, it means that instead of having one task that you work on till the end, that you have several in various stages of completion. While you're waiting for something to simmer on the stove, for example, you can be rinsing dishes and loading them in the dishwasher. While you're on hold on the phone, you are straightening your work area. While you're waiting for paint to dry in one area of your house, you might be prepping the next. The list of tasks that can be done simultaneously is endless.

Where this gets tricky is when you have lots of half-completed tasks, and nothing gets completely done. To balance, you need to monitor yourself and stop multitasking when you have too many tasks going at once. Try to determine what your limit of tasks "in progress" is. Is it three? Two? Is it better for you to only focus on one?

Task Switching

Task switching means working on one task, and, as you lose momentum, moving on to a different task. Simply making a change can be invigorating, and you'll be able to accomplish more than you would by forcing yourself to slog through the first task. At a future time, you can switch back to the first project, coming back to it with a renewed sense of purpose and energy.

The drawback of this technique is similar to the one above—that you end up with lots of half-completed projects. This is especially likely if you have a tendency toward distraction and wandering off before you are finished. The new and novel are generally lots more fun than the job you're doing now. To balance, switch between only two projects at a time. You can still take advantage of the energy rush of working on something different, but you'll eventually get them both done.

The Downside of Multitasking

There is no question that multitasking can be a very good thing. It can increase your efficiency and help you to take advantage of those spare bits of time that occur during the day. My concern is that it can also keep you from ever being fully present in any situation. When you're out walking, you're also on the phone. When you're on the phone, you're cleaning the kitchen. When you're with your children, you're cleaning out a drawer. These can be good uses of your time. But you can multitask your way through life without having really *lived*. Multitasking is good, but it must be balanced with activities that take your full attention and even with downtime when you're really not accomplishing anything. Balance will keep this technique in check so it doesn't become the driving, manic force in your life.

• 32 •
Simplifying Your Holidays

While songs claim that the winter holiday season is "the most wonderful time of the year," many people actually dread this period. Of all the winter holidays, Christmas is often the most challenging. There is so much to do. We eat too much, spend too much, and feel guilty if the holiday season is not nonstop delight. My Jewish friends tell me that Hanukkah is getting similarly out of hand. And many families celebrate both!

You might expect that in a book on household organization, I would tell you how to be more efficient with your time so that you can cram it all in. Instead, I'm going to suggest that you prune, and keep only what you enjoy. Here are some steps to have a simplified and more meaningful holiday.

Make Conscious Choices

You are offered an array of activities during the holiday season, and you may run from one activity to another, not really enjoying any of them. It's far better if you can pick the ones that are most meaningful to you. Be honest with yourself. Do you really enjoy baking? Holiday cards? Matching outfits for everyone? Home decorations that look like Martha Stewart is stopping by? If your answer is yes, then, by all means, continue. If the answer is no, however, then drop activities you don't like. Or assign them to someone else. Discuss your holiday activities with your family and see which activities can be eliminated, modified, or temporarily put on hold because of your current situation or the needs of your family.

Keep Your Expectations Realistic

You shouldn't expect week upon week of unending happiness during the holidays. If you expect this of yourself, you are bound to be disappointed. There will be ups and downs just like during the rest of the year. Nor should you expect your home, family, and yourself to look and behave like the mythic creatures on television and in magazines. It's not fair for you or your kids.

Spread Activities over Time

Another option is to spread the activities out over a period of time. For example, can you send holiday cards in January? Can you have a holiday party during the summer? There is no reason to cram all of our social obligations into the period between Thanksgiving and New Year's.

Spend within Your Means

A major source of holiday stress is spending too much, especially when most of us have too much junk anyway. To trim back, you can approach others on your gift list to see if they would like to do the same. Can you draw names? Can you agree to only give gifts to the kids? While some may not want to make these changes, you might find that others are also feeling overwhelmed by the holidays and are thrilled that you made the suggestion.

Let's all resolve to make conscious choices about how much we want to do this year. Everyone in our lives will notice a difference. And maybe this year, the holidays can be fun for you, too!

• PART V •

Get Rid of Clutter

• 33 •
Finding a Good Home for Your Stuff

We all hang on to things we don't need because we paid good money for them and don't want to just throw them away. I can totally relate. But I have also found a cure—finding a good home for your stuff. So here are some ways to pass along your prized possessions.

Give It to Friends

If you don't like a particular product or item, perhaps someone you know will. It never hurts to ask. Ditto with clothing that's in good shape but doesn't look good on you. Sometimes it can be fun to bring together a group of friends and have a "free" yard sale. People bring what they don't need, and others can help themselves.

If you have children, families with children younger than yours often appreciate books, toys, and clothes that are still in good shape. When giving away these types of items, ask ahead of time if your friends would like them. Sometimes families are already inundated with items, and you don't want to contribute to someone else's clutter.

Find a Worthy Cause

It's easier to give stuff away if you know that it will go to help others. For example, it's often easier to part with that extra set of dishes, sheets, or towels when they're going to a shelter and helping someone start a new life. Do you know someone who is just starting out on their own? Chances are, they would be thrilled to have some of your stuff. And what about those business suits that are too nice to just give to the Salvation Army? You can try a consignment shop, or you can donate them to a program called Dressed for Success. It provides business attire to low-income people who are interviewing for jobs.

Verizon collects old cell phones to give to women escaping from battering relationships. Lenscrafters and the Lions Club collect old prescription glasses that they give to low-income people. Maternity clothes and baby gear can go to a local pregnancy center. In colder climates, many elementary and middle schools collect kids' winter gear to give to children whose families cannot afford it. Libraries are often thrilled to get books, CDs, videos, and magazines that you no longer need. If in doubt, ask before you bring stuff over. Most of these donations are also tax deductible and can add up to hundreds of dollars in deductions. If you plan to take deductions, be sure to get receipts and keep lists of the items that you donate.

A Word of Caution

I have one warning. Don't hang on to your stuff for too long. Libraries are much less inclined to take your fifteen-year-old paperbacks with yellowed pages. Clothes and shoes that are ten years out-of-date also can be a problem. I used to collect baby gear and clothing for our local pregnancy center. It was heartbreaking when we had to throw away car seats that were older than five years (the plastic deteriorates and would not hold up in a crash). While you don't necessarily want to give away items the moment you are finished with them, you don't want to hang on forever, either.

Finding a good home for your belongings is the ultimate win-win situation. You get rid of clutter and get tax deductions. The recipient gets what they need without having to spend a lot of money. And our society wins because these surplus items don't end up in a landfill. Don't you have something that you would like to share?

• 34 •

Your Bedroom: Dungeon or Oasis?

Many people I talk with tell me that their bedrooms are often piled with mail, mounds of clothing, toys, books and magazines they haven't read, exercise equipment they don't use, and various types of pocket debris. In short, their bedrooms have become the depository for all the junk in the house.

I would like to propose something that may seem radical. Rather than letting your bedroom become a junkyard for the rest of your home, make your bedroom a priority. I have valid health reasons for making such a suggestion. According to the National Sleep Foundation, sleep problems are rampant in this country, and fatigue is taking a toll on the health of our nation. Part of the problem lies in poor sleeping habits, and some of these can be traced back to using our bedroom as a portable office, playpen, laundry-sorting area, and storage space. A cluttered, messy room is stressful to enter at the end of the day and stressful to wake up in. Here are some simple suggestions for making your bedroom a place of calm.

Make Your Bed Every Morning

Making your bed can be your first pocket of order in an otherwise messy room. It provides a place to start cleaning and will give you a surface to work on. This task should only take a couple of minutes. If it takes longer, simplify your bedding and move any furniture that is blocking your way.

Be Able to Store All of Your Clothing All at Once

Make sure that you have sufficient space for your clothing. Right now, that might seem impossible. But when you follow the suggestions in some of the other chapters in this book, you'll have sorted your clothes and can make this suggestion a reality.

Make Your Room Easy to Clean

Be sure to have a trash can and laundry hamper either in your room or nearby. If you have clothing that must be dry cleaned, consider a separate hamper for these items so that they don't accidentally end up in the wash.

Avoid Working in Your Bedroom

Sometimes, this is unavoidable. If you must work in your bedroom, cover your workspace at night when you're not working. It can also be stressful to have an overflowing end table with books to read and magazines you never get to. All this does is remind you of work that you never seem to have time to finish. If you are having sleep troubles, stash your mound of reading materials out of sight.

A Word about Pocket Change

A recent statistic indicated that most people have at least seventy dollars in change lying around their house, unused. This is wasteful and, frankly, kind of dumb. Much of the change from your house is likely to end up in your room. Have some way of collecting it in a cup or dish, and cash it in from time to time. I have a coin sorter in my top drawer. There is a separate tube for each type of coin. When the tubes fill up, I put the coins in a coin roll. When I have collected a certain number of these, I take them to the bank. I usually have fifty to sixty dollars in change. My family and I use this money to go do something fun.

An organized, peaceful bedroom can be a tremendous advantage. You'll sleep better, and the beginning of each day will be more pleasant. As you make progress in this room, reward yourself with some pretty sheets and maybe a new bedspread, too. That can be an extra incentive for you to make your bed.

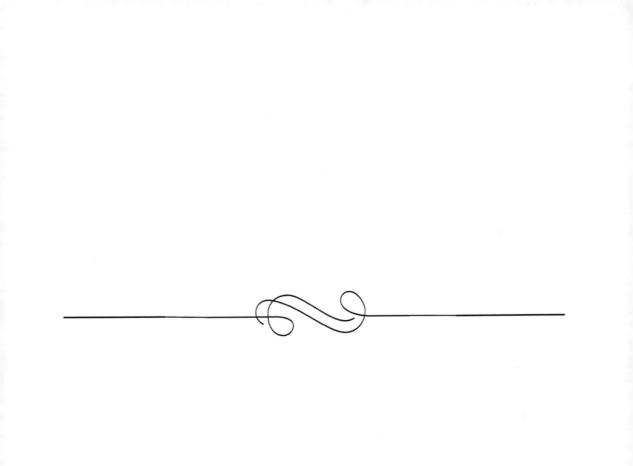

• 35 •
Making the Most of Drawer Space

Drawers are probably our most badly used type of storage space. Most homes are short on these, and yet they are often used to store the most inappropriate types of stuff. Messy drawers can drain hours from your life. It's so easy for small items to get lost, and it's hard to find what you need. I propose two goals for your drawers that might seem tough at first: (1) be able to open and close drawers easily, and (2) be able see what is inside at a glance. These are attainable goals if you get rid of clutter and treat them as active storage.

Pull Anything That Doesn't Belong

As you begin to sort your drawers, pull out anything that is awkward or that catches when you open or close. In a kitchen, for my example, many people use their drawers to store things like serving spoons. I don't recommend that because of their awkward sizes and shapes. For these items, a crock or container by the side of the stove is better. You can see what you have, and they won't become a jumble in your drawers.

Location, Location, Location

Think about your work areas and what you want to accomplish there, then plan your drawers accordingly. Drawers near your sink or dishwasher should contain your silverware; drawers near your stove, your pot holders; drawers near your bathroom mirror, your cosmetics. You get the idea.

Use Active Storage

Put the items you use often toward the front and in the middle, the items you use less

The Well-Ordered Home

often toward the back and on the sides. Remove anything that you don't use on a regular basis. Items you use less frequently need to go somewhere else, especially if drawer space is scarce.

Use Storage Devices

Drawers can become a colossal mess in a hurry. Fortunately, there are lots of storage devices for inside your drawers. That's good. The more dividers and storage units you use, the easier it will be to see what you have inside. You'll especially need containers or compartments for small items that get bounced around when you open and close drawers. If your contents tend to slide a lot, you can get rubber mats that fit under your storage containers. These keep everything in place.

If you don't already have one, get a good rack for your silverware. Most silverware racks are solid on the bottom. Unfortunately, crumbs and other food debris often fall into your drawers and accumulate in the bottom of your rack. You might consider getting one made from wire or plastic mesh (Target sells these) so that crumbs don't accumulate in it. To clean out the crumbs, you simply lift out the rack and clean under it (meaning you don't have to remove your silverware to clean it). For other drawers, shallow baskets or other small containers work well. Rubbermaid sells interlocking baskets of various sizes. These can be used to accommodate most drawers. You can get special inserts to hold your knives in drawers. And don't forget to look in office-supply stores. There are many convenient storage devices that work well in odd-shaped drawers. These will help you see what is in your drawer at a glance. For deeper drawers, you might find that plastic baskets work well. These can be helpful for sorting socks and underwear.

Tidy drawers will pay you back every single day. Once you've tried it, you'll never go back to the way things were.

• 36 •
Family Memories: Sorting through Photos

If your house was on fire and you could only grab one thing, chances are it would be your family photos. It's amazing that something only the wealthy could afford a hundred years ago has become such an integral part of family life. Family photos are also, in most households, an organization nightmare. Fortunately, there are some simple steps you can take.

Gather All Your Photos in One Place

Start by gathering all your pictures. This might take minutes or days depending on the amount and state of your photos. But it's an important step to sorting and putting them together in some type of meaningful order.

Sort by Approximate Date

If the pictures are not marked or date stamped, you may have to guess based on outfits, hairstyles, pets, and household items that are in the picture. As you are sorting by date, dump pictures that are blurry, out of focus, or that chop off heads. You might also consider dumping (or at least setting aside) pictures of people you don't know. Time is unlikely to improve your memory. If you don't know who these people are, why keep the picture?

Group into a Logical Order

Are there a series of pictures of a specific occasion? Do you recognize a particular year? Were any from a particular trip or vacation? As you work, try to make your categories more and more narrow. You may find that it takes several days for you to sort through everything. This can be a fun activity for other family members, too. You might also consider doing the sorting when you have a longer stretch of time, such as during a relaxing vacation or while you're recovering from an illness.

Decide about Storage and Display

The good (and bad) news is that you have lots of options. Do you want to put photos in an album, or would a storage box with partitions work better? Are all your pictures roughly the same size, or do you have multiple sizes? Multiple sizes may require that you use a magnetic album rather than one with sleeves. Only use acid-free boxes and albums so that your photos don't deteriorate.

When you have decided between an album or box, get out your labeler and go to work. Clearly label the categories and year (if you know it) in either the album or on the box partitions. Label the outside of the boxes and albums, too. Gently label the back of the photos with either a Sharpie ink marker or a graphite pencil (available at craft and art-supply stores). Don't use a ballpoint pen because it will show through.

Some Final Thoughts

Make sure that you store your photos in a place that is neither too hot nor too cold (like hot attics or freezing garages). Also be careful about exposing them to sunlight, since this can ruin them. Finally, think about storing some of your pictures or negatives in another location just in case something happens to your home. Give copies to relatives, keep some negatives in your safe-deposit box, or copy them to disk. Your family photos cannot be replaced. Make sure yours are safe.

• 37 •
Mastering the Chilly Abyss

In most American homes, there is a large refrigerator crammed with perishable food. Unfortunately, we end up wasting a tremendous amount of it because food spoils before we can eat it. This is an issue my family has struggled with, and it's made me wonder if storing so much food is really a good idea. As a culture, we shop less frequently for food than our forebears. Before people had refrigerators, families shopped every day or so for perishables, and vendors brought food directly to our homes. Because we must now drive to the supermarket, the average person or family now shops less frequently and buys more per visit. Here are some suggestions to help you eat what you buy.

Start where you are. Buy for how you actually eat rather than how you think you should. For example, I think we all agree that it's a good idea to eat produce. But you need to be realistic about how much produce you and your family will eat in a given week. Produce is often the first thing to go bad. It doesn't make sense to buy lots of it if you never eat at home. You may eventually want to make changes in your diet or eat at home more often. But don't shop now like you're already doing that.

Buy things you like and know how to prepare. Food sometimes goes bad because we never have the time to figure out how to cook it. So it simply sits until it's unusable. Unless you plan to figure out how to cook it *today,* don't buy it.

Eat by the seasons. We have a system of transport that brings us fresh produce year round. This is truly amazing, when you think about it. It's often difficult to tell from the produce aisle what time of year that it is. But *you* can tell. Start becoming aware of when foods are in season. Out-of-season foods are more expensive, are often tasteless because they have to be picked so early, and may be days or weeks old by the time you get them.

Shipping from long distances has a negative impact on the environment. Also, it stands to reason that older food won't last as long at your house. Fruits and vegetables that are in season are likely to be fresher and will last longer.

Know what's in your refrigerator. So often, things go bad because we forget that they are there. That's a shame. Every couple of days, take a look through your refrigerator and determine what you need to eat in the next day or so. This appraisal includes taking a spin through the condiments and other oddball stuff that ends up in the door or drawers.

Have a periodic smorgasbord night. This is the night when you eat all the little dabs of stuff that may be left over from the week. This can be fun, and it's essentially free food. Also, you'll find that a lot fewer things go bad when there is a regular turnover of leftovers.

By being more selective about your food choices, your refrigerator becomes less crowded. You can see what you have and make sure you use what you've bought. You save money by wasting less food, and will have mastered the chilly abyss.

• 38 •
Conquering the Frozen Wasteland

In the preceding chapter, I described how our refrigerators are often a source of waste. We buy too much and can't eat it all before it goes bad. Our freezers aren't much better. We have this attitude that food will remain forever in its cryogenic state, and that we can drag it out and eat it even a year or more later. The freezer often becomes the never-never land of remnants that we can't bring ourselves to dump but don't really want to eat either. I'm not sure that this is a good strategy.

Don't get me wrong. Freezers can be essential for both organization and thrift. You can store food that is ready to heat and serve when you and your family reach a particularly busy time. And freezers can allow you to stock up on meats and other items when they are on sale.

But freezers only work effectively when there is a regular turnover of the food in them. Contrary to popular belief, frozen food will not keep forever. Six months is about as long as you'll want to keep it. After that, food picks up odors, gets freezer burn, and just starts tasting nasty. You can freeze and store hundreds of dollars worth of food that no one, with the possible exception of your dog, will eat. The other option is to use your freezer wisely. Here are some suggestions.

Start where you are. If you don't usually eat dinner at home, it doesn't make sense to spend huge quantities of money on frozen foods. You'll just end up throwing it out when it sits too long in the freezer, and you may find yourself reluctant to try again. Start with small amounts and foods you already buy (beyond ice cream). You can build from there.

Be realistic about what you decide to store. Sometimes, we just can't bring ourselves to throw away food, even if it's positively yucky. Freezing rarely improves the taste. It's probably better to dump, compost, or give it to the dog.

Keep a mental (or actual) list of what is in your freezer. Mark the date on items you freeze, and then get in the habit of using the older food first. Label anything that isn't obvious. You can purchase stickers for your plastic containers so you can label those. Keep a waterproof ink marker near your freezer so you can do this easily.

Have a periodic leftovers feast night. Just like with your refrigerator, you have one night every few weeks when you eat leftovers from the freezer. You can also plan weekly menus by the foods that need to be eaten soon. You'll find fewer mysteries freezer-burned beyond recognition when there is regular turnover.

Like your refrigerator, your freezer can be a wonderful tool that allows you to store food for a future time, save money, and be able to pull out a meal that simply needs to be heated—a real godsend on a crazy day. By being more selective about what you choose to store, your freezer becomes less crowded, making regular turnover of items easier to accomplish. You can see what you have, use what you have purchased, and conquer the frozen wasteland.

• 39 •

Finding Your "Look" Will Do Wonders for Your Closet

Clothing is a major storage issue—especially for women. To organize your clothing, you must first discover what looks good on you and what you like to wear. Women, in particular, can be funny shoppers. We're often influenced by price or current style, rather than what we like or what looks good on us. We shop when we are tired or bored, and haul home a strange variety of items. We keep things that are too small or that we never liked (but paid good money for). Then we end up having tons of clothes, but quite literally, nothing to wear.

Knowing what looks good can make you a more effective shopper. This is something I discovered years ago with bathing suits. There is one style that is best for me. The rest look pretty bad in comparison. This little revelation has shortened my shopping time and saved me lots of money. Keeping my best look in mind has been helpful with other clothing items as well.

Once you know what your best look is, you can start making decisions about what to keep and what to pass along to someone else. Consider the following.

What Are Your Preferences?

- What type of fabrics do you like?

- What brands do you like?

- Do you reach for the same couple of outfits day after day? What is it about those that you like so much?

- What outfits tend to get a lot of compliments?

- What do you feel good wearing?

- What colors look good on you?

- What other criteria are important to you?

Mine are fairly simple. I like clothing that is comfortable (and that includes shoes). I prefer 100 percent cotton in most things, I like things that I don't have to dry clean, and I want fabrics that don't wrinkle easily. But you'll come up with your own list. You also need to be realistic about types of clothes you need for work. These may need to be dressier than you would normally wear. But even within this narrow range, there will be items that look particularly good on you.

It may take some time until you have a good sense of what types of clothing you like. Once you get it, however, your shopping will be dramatically simplified. You will no longer waste your time on clothing that is not "you" (for example, I rarely try on anything with ruffles). You'll become less likely to run out and get this year's "must have" unless it is a style that really works for you. You will spend less money in the long run because you always have something that looks nice for any occasion. And you will actually wear what you buy because it all looks good.

Once you have your style in mind, it's time to hit your closet—the subject of the next chapter.

• 40 •
Getting in the Closet

Now that you have a good idea of what style fits you, it's time to tackle your closet. My current closet is about two feet wide (in an old house). These principles have served me well. Hopefully, you have more space to work with.

Clearing Out the Center of Your Closet

This is your active storage space. Only put clothes in this space that currently fit, that you like to wear, and that you wear often. As you do, group by type: all short-sleeved shirts put together; all long-sleeved shirts in the same area; and so forth. Depending on how well you've shopped for yourself over the years, this section may have a nice selection of clothes, or may have only a few. We'll worry about that later.

If you have outfits that you wear only occasionally, but would still like to keep handy, put these in on one side. If there is room, you can put your seasonal clothing (like winter clothes if it's summer) on the other side. If there isn't room, box these up and store them elsewhere (for instance, the attic, basement, or under your bed).

Now Let's Look at the Rest

Grab each item and try to determine why you're not wearing it. We all have a tendency to save clothing that is too small with the hopes that "someday" we'll fit back into it. I don't mean to discourage you, but how realistic is that? If you are currently losing weight, it's realistic. If, however, you are like most of us, "losing weight" is on the to-do list, but not likely in the near future. In that case, clothing that is too small needs to be either given away or packed elsewhere. At the very least, these items need to be out of your active storage.

Pull out the precious little numbers you bought and never wear. Either give these away or take them to a consignment store (some may still have the price tags on them). That goes for clothing that other people gave you, items that you picked up on vacation, and items you bought while temporarily insane.

Finding the Gems

When sorting this pile, you need to be discerning. Within these mounds of clothing, there may be some gems—something that fits well, is attractive, and would work in your wardrobe, but is missing a key component. Maybe it needs to be altered or needs a special bra. Make it a point in the next week to make these garments wearable. Then put them in your active storage.

Clothing on Probation

By now, you should have whittled your pile down quite a bit. The final category to consider is the items that you're just not sure of. Let's call this pile "on probation." If you are not sure about an item, take it out for a test drive. Wear it, and try to figure out why you never do. It could be that it's great, and it just got buried. If that's the case, move it to active storage. In other cases, you'll usually know within a pretty short time. Maybe it pinches as the day goes on or looks like you slept in it after wearing it for a few minutes. Or maybe it has gone out of style. (Hint: if someone asks you if you wore it to your prom, it's probably out of date!) On the other hand, if it is out of style and you still like it—wear it anyway! You'll be a trendsetter. Who ever thought that tie-dye would make a comeback?

• 41 •

Sorting through Accessories

Now that your hanging clothes are in good shape, let's get the rest of your clothing squared away. We need to make sure that you have what you need and that we trim away the excess (think Imelda Marcos).

Socks, bras, underwear, and other items. Start by grouping all similar items together. You may consider adding some storage baskets inside your drawers to keep things neat. Discard any underwear with holes, elastic that is shot, or that is badly stained (no one wants these). Ditto with bras that are uncomfortable, always ride up, or that have straps that fall down. Get rid of socks that don't fit or that are badly worn, and panty hose with runs. (Please don't tell me that one leg is still good.) Do you have everything you need? If not, start acquiring necessary items as your budget permits. If you wear panty hose, always keep at least one extra pair on hand.

Purses. Women tend to have a lot of these. Unless you are actively using them all, it might be good to thin the herd. You might even consider having just one everyday purse and one or two dress purses. But that is strictly your call. Make sure that you have at least one really functional purse.

Scarves, belts, and necklaces. These also tend to proliferate. To keep them useable, store them where you can easily see them. I have all three on a rack on my closet door. I can see what I have in a snap, and can tell if I am not wearing it for some reason. Pare them down periodically to keep your collection current.

Shoes. This tends to be a big category for many women. I'm not going to suggest that you pare down to three pair of shoes (horrors!). But shoes can be a storage challenge. Put the shoes you wear a lot into your active storage. You can probably pull shoes that are seasonal and store them with your winter or summer clothes. You can also pull shoes that are for special occasions, and put them somewhere else (like with your special-occasion clothing). The shoes that remain now need to be sorted. Put them on probation like you did with your clothing. Give serious thought to getting rid of anything that hurts your feet. You don't want to pay later with bunions, bad knees, or bad hips because you kept wearing shoes that hurt (no matter how fabulous they looked).

Chest of drawers. The final area to tackle is your chest of drawers. Make it a goal to be able to put all your clothing away at the same time while also managing to open and close your drawers with ease. Start by pulling all your seasonal clothing and storing it elsewhere. Then keep everything you wear a lot right where you can grab it. Sort the rest accordingly.

Shopping in your storage area. What if you sort everything, and you just don't have room for all the great clothes you have? Well, one solution is to put most of it in your active storage area and store the excess. As you start wearing clothing in your active storage more regularly, it may actually wear out. Instead of hitting the mall, grab a box of your stored clothing. You'll find some wonderful items, and it won't cost you a dime. Plus you'll have freed up lots of storage space, too.

Sorting through your clothes and accessories can free up space and save you time every morning. Since these items are more accessible, you may also find that you wear a greater variety of outfits as well. You save space and look great, too!

• 42 •

Simplified Grooming:
Changing Your Routines

I recently read an article about women who had decided to simplify their hair. Most had been doing some fairly dramatic things—lightening dark hair, straightening curly hair, curling straight hair. They decided to save time and money by letting their hair go natural. The women in the article all explained that the look they were trying so hard to maintain was no longer *them*.

Likewise, your grooming routines might need some consideration, particularly if your morning routine is rushed. Grooming also accounts for time away from home for perms, color, cuts, or manicures. The commitment in terms of both time and money can be enormous.

I want to be very clear: personal grooming choices are yours alone. Some people who have embraced the simplicity movement have been against hair products, makeup, and nail polish, which is fine if that's what they want to do. But they can't tell *you* to get rid of these things, too. What you cut and what you keep in your routine is nobody's business but your own. In looking at your routines, you might decide that you like them all. In that case, don't change a thing. But there may be some things you can cut.

Hair

Can you have a haircut that doesn't need to be curled? If you color your hair, would it look better closer to its natural color or a color that doesn't take so much work (maybe a little darker so the roots aren't so obvious)? If your hair is permed or colored, could you do it yourself? If your hairstyle is short and needs frequent trims to stay looking good, could you have a slightly longer style that needs less maintenance?

Nails

In some parts of the country, an unmanicured nail is almost gauche. In other parts (like New Hampshire), no one thinks twice. A manicure is totally wasted on me. I tend to ruin it in less than twenty-four hours because I'm always digging around in something (and forget to put on gloves). But I know women who *love* having manicured nails. For them, a manicure is totally worth it. It's up to you. If you like having polished nails, could you do it yourself? Does it make more sense to polish your toenails and leave your fingernails *au naturel*?

Makeup

Some makeup routines can be pretty involved, and this may be worth it on special occasions. But for your daily routine, you might want to simplify things. It may already be trimmed down, but occasionally, it's good to examine all your routines and see if they can be improved.

These suggestions are meant to accomplish several things. They are meant to help you find your best look in hair, makeup, and nails. They're also meant to help you locate areas where you might be able to save some time, especially in your morning routine. And finally, once you are clear about your grooming routine, it will help you clear up another major source of household clutter: grooming implements and supplies—the subject of the next chapter.

• 43 •

Simplified Grooming:
Your Supplies and Implements

In the previous chapter, I described how you could trim your grooming routine. Being organized is not about depriving yourself of routines that you find enjoyable or that make you feel attractive. It's about knowing and honoring what works best for you, and discarding parts that are time-consuming and no longer work. Hair, nail, and makeup products can be a significant source of clutter in your bathroom, under your sink, and in your medicine cabinet. Paring down these items will free up space and save you time in your daily grooming routines.

Hair Supplies

Bathroom counters and drawers often become archives of our past styles and products that didn't work. The problem is only multiplied when there are multiple members of a household.

Electrical hair implements. With each new hairstyle, you may get a different electrical implement: curling irons, hair dryers, hair straighteners, hair crimpers, and electric rollers. Realistically consider whether you need them all or are likely to go back to a hairstyle that will require these.

Other hair implements. These include rollers, bobby pins, hairpins, clips, barrettes, head bands, and a whole host of hair decorations. Again, I wouldn't necessary get rid of all of these, but ask yourself whether you're likely to go back to a style that uses these or whether they reflect who you are now.

Hair products. If you have products that you are not using, would you use them if stored in a more convenient place? If you know that you definitely would not use them, do you know someone who could? Homeless shelters may take them. They can also use little shampoos and conditioners that come from hotels. The rest of the products you may have to just dump (I know it's hard). Or you may be able to figure out another use for them (like using shampoo for hand washable items).

Nails

If you polish your nails, your stash of nail polish could probably use some pruning. Dump any polish you have that is dried, clumpy, or just plain ugly. (Before throwing any liquid polish or polish remover in the trash, see if this qualifies as hazardous waste in your city or town.) I make periodic sweeps through my stash of polish and give away any that is too "teenage" for me (that includes most shades of green and blue). Dump or give away broken nail files, emery boards, cuticle removers, press-on nails, and polish remover you don't like.

Makeup

Your makeup collection can be another chronicle of poor choices: foundation that is too orange, eye shadow that creases or smears, mascara that always looks clumpy. You're probably going to have to dump most of this stuff. Anything that comes in contact with your lips, eyes, or skin can pick up bacteria. If in doubt about a product, try it for a day and see what happens. You may discover that it's great. On the other hand, you may discover exactly why you never wear it. That will make the decision pretty easy.

Paring down your grooming supplies will cut time from your grooming routine. You'll save money since you'll no longer buy stuff you don't need. And you'll look good, too!

· 44 ·
Attacking "The Pile"

I was recently speaking at parenting conference. A group of moms suddenly started talking about "the pile." They all confessed that they had one and wanted to know what to do about it. If you don't know what I am talking about, you don't need to read this chapter. Chances are, however, you know *exactly* what I'm talking about. Most families handle huge amounts of paper. Ignore it for a couple of days, and you have a pile. Ignore it for a couple of months, and it will cover most of your dining room table. This problem may be a minor or major crisis, depending on how long it has been since you have handled your paper. The good news is that you *can* dig your way out.

Preparing for Your Attack

The pile before you might seem overwhelming. But like anything, you can work on it a bit at a time. Set up a mail-sorting area and assemble your supplies. These include a letter opener, envelopes, return-address stickers, stamps, paper clips or a stapler, a paper-recycling bin, a razor knife, and a place to file.

Your First Pass Through

You're probably familiar with old adage that you should only handle paper once. I'm going to ask you to break that, at least for now. First, pull out anything that is clearly junk. That can reduce your pile quite a bit. Be sure to open every envelope, though. Many times, I've opened what I assumed was junk only to find a check, my new credit card, or something else that I wanted. Toss all the junk into your recycling bin.

Handling What's Left

Envelopes. On your next pass, grab all the envelopes that you didn't get the first time. Open everything and then sort it: bills, activities, things that need a response, and junk. Recycle the junk. Put your bills in a stack to be paid. Record any activities on your calendar, and respond to items that need a response.

After you have grabbed and dealt with all the envelopes, you can be more leisurely about the rest of your sorting. Grab an inch or so to sort while watching TV. Bring a stack when you have some waiting to do or have a long ride in a car (assuming you are a passenger).

Catalogs. Most of these can go. If you are sure that you'll need something from it, save *one* from each company. As you get a new one, recycle the outdated one.

Periodicals. These can be the last thing to sort through. Fight the temptation to read through the whole stack of these. If it is something you keep (like a journal), skim through it and put it on your shelf. For other publications, scan through and see if there are any articles you want to read. Cut these out and put them in your "read" pile. Recycle the rest. Also decide whether you want to keep receiving a periodical that you never have time to read. Popular magazines that you haven't cut up can go to the library or your local school. They are often thrilled to have these (ask first). Otherwise, they can be recycled.

Sorting through your pile can take hours or days, depending on how long it's been accumulating. But as you chip away at it, before you know it, you'll have conquered the pile. And anytime it starts accumulating again, you can use the same strategy.

• 45 •
Handling Paper As It Comes In

Now that you have a handle on your backlog, it's time to deal with the incoming mail so that it doesn't get stacked up again. In order to do that, you will need to set up a mail station. Picture yourself coming home, mail in hand. Where do you tend to land? Chances are, your best place to set up a mail station is near there.

Assemble your supplies. If you haven't already done so, assemble some of the basic tools: a letter opener, stamps, envelopes, return-address labels, a razor knife, a recycling bin, and a place to file. You will also need to have your master calendar handy. Ready?

Open everything. Just like when you handled your backlog, I would encourage you to grab all the envelopes first and open each one. Some of these will be junk. But you can't always tell, and it's better to be safe than sorry.

Pull out any bills first. Open them, remove the inserts, and stack the bills and return envelopes in your "bills" pile. These will need to be transported to the area where you pay bills (which may be where you are or in another location).

Grab anything that looks like an event. Record the date on your master calendar, along with any additional information you need, such as directions or items you are asked to bring. Jot down the return address and toss the envelope. Toss the announcement or save it near your calendar. Open envelopes with notes or other things that need a response from you. Either respond now, or put it in a place where you can respond to several things at once.

Skim through flyers and junk mail. Cut out or mark things that are of interest, and recycle the rest. Skim through catalogs, too. Keep them only if you anticipate really ordering something. Then only keep the most current (or biggest, if those come out periodically). Recycle the rest.

Look at your magazines and newsletters. Sort through the ones you want to read. Set them in a place where you are likely to read them. After you're finished with them, recycle or donate them. If more than six months or so pass, and you still haven't read them, glance through to see if there are any articles you simply *must* read. If so, cut them out and recycle the rest. Add the articles to your "read" pile. Keep this handy so you can use spare bits of time to go through it. If months go by and you still haven't read it, you might consider tossing it. Remember that you don't have to keep up on every bit of news. Give yourself permission to let some of it go. And if you are noticing that you *never* seem to get around to reading a certain publication, it might make sense for you to cancel it or let it expire. Remember, too, that libraries often have magazines you can check out. If you need a magazine fix, you can get one for free, and they won't be cluttering up your home.

Sort it every day. Get in the habit of sorting the mail as soon as you can. Every day is preferable. This will be easier to do if you have set up a system that allows you to easily sort your mail and file what is left.

Handling mail as it comes in will keep you from getting buried. Do it regularly, and it takes a lot less time. At the very least, your pile won't get any bigger. Or better yet, you can keep one from developing at all.

• 46 •
Filing 101

Once you have gone through your piles and have developed a strategy for handling your mail, you need to find a way to store all the stuff you decide to save. The main thing is that you want to be able to find it once you put it away. Piles often serve as running to-do lists. We have a tendency to leave stuff out so we won't forget to do something about it. Unfortunately, that is a pretty inefficient system. It's much better to develop a filing system that works and track things you need to do in your date book or electronic organizer. Here are some simple rules to help guide your filing.

Designate a place. Decide where you are going to keep your files. They can be in the filing cabinet, a desk drawer, a deco file or portable filing box, or a portfolio. If you're not sure, try a couple of different setups and see what works for you. Then decide.

Less is more. A frequent mistake is making a filing system much too complex. You don't want to have many little categories when a few broad ones will do. Some possibilities are a separate folder for everyone in the family. Any paperwork pertaining to that person can go in that file, including school paperwork, health records, and activity rosters. You could also make categories by type of information: health records, receipts, credit cards, car, school, memberships, or activities. If you find that these categories are too big, you can break them down. But often, you'll find that these categories work well, letting you locate the information you need.

A system that works well for me is to have a Pendaflex folder for each month. I frequently book conferences and meetings as much as a year in advance. When I get information on these meetings, I enter it in my Palm Pilot, start a folder, and file it under the appropriate month. I can always find it when I need it.

Make your files pretty. If you make your filing system attractive and easy to use, you are more likely to use it. Fortunately, filing equipment now comes in a wide range of colors and styles. Your files will look so great that you'll *want* to use them.

Use active storage. If you are doing your filing in a small space, you will want to only keep the most current files at hand. Files that are more than a year old should be stored elsewhere. This includes tax records and other information you are required to keep for the IRS. These can be stored in an attic, closet, or other more out-of-the-way space.

Learning to handle paperwork well will help in every area of your life. You can find what you need, and you won't have to leave it laying around in piles.

• 47 •
Handling Financial Papers

Money may make the world go 'round, but most of us have a hard time handling our financial papers. Unfortunately, ignorance is not bliss in this case and could lead to financial hardship. Learning to handle your financial papers is essential.

Assemble All Your Papers

If you haven't already done so, gather your papers from around your home. This includes bank statements, credit-card statements, statements from investment accounts, tax returns, and all your receipts.

Pull All Current Bills

First things first. Pay your bills. Decide which part of your home will be your bill-paying area. Decide on a spot for bills, and use that for bills alone. As you open your mail each day, add any bills to this folder, along with their envelopes.

Then decide how often you are going to pay bills. It could be once a week, once every two weeks, or once a month (note that some bills come due faster than once a month). Be religious about this date. If you keep up on your bills, you'll find it won't take as long as it has in the past.

If you are comfortable using a computer, you might check out the option of paying your bills online. This is quick and easy and allows you to keep track of money in your bank accounts, too. Many banks offer this option free of charge. But remembering the principle of start where you are, only explore this option if you are comfortable on a computer. If you've gotten into a good routine with paying your bills, you are ready to take the next step.

Develop Files for Financial Papers

To get a handle on your money and where it is, you need to create a filing system for your financial papers. Create a hanging folder for each of these categories.

- **Tax documents.** Create a separate file folder for each year's tax return along with any tax documents for that year. The IRS requires that you keep your tax returns for seven years.

- **Retirement accounts.** Keep your statements from any retirement accounts. Have a separate folder for each account.

- **Investments.** Keep statements from any investments that are not retirement accounts.

- **Bank accounts.** Have a separate folder for each checking or savings account, and keep monthly statements from each.

- **Debts.** Keep monthly statements for each credit card in a separate folder. Also have a folder for each car and any student loans that are outstanding.

- **Homeowner accounts.** Have a separate folder for your house title, home improvements, and mortgage.

- **Insurance policies.** File each insurance policy here, including health, life, car, homeowners, and disability.

This filing system will allow you to make informed decisions about your money, perhaps for the first time. You can't go wrong!

• 48 •
Making the Most of What You Have

At first blush, this may not sound like an organizational tip. But as you will see, when we learn to make the most of what we have, we are better able to resist the temptation to bring more in. Stopping the massive inflow of stuff saves money and takes us much closer to our goal of creating a serene space.

Clear Up Clutter

There is wisdom in the "less is more" adage. When your home is crammed, individual pieces get lost. I've been in homes with beautiful antiques that you could barely see, let alone appreciate, because they were buried in debris. Dejunking provides a breath of fresh air throughout your home.

Move Stuff Around

Sometimes, we shop and bring new stuff home when we are bored with what we have. Every March, I get so sick of winter and am dying for something new. But I've learned to first try to do some new things with what I have. The fact of the matter is that we habituate to things that we see all the time. When you start getting bored and have the urge to go buy something, try moving a picture, lamp, or other item to a new location. Moving what you already have can do wonders.

Use Principles of Interior Design

Grouping objects together can draw attention to them in new ways. Have a focal point in every room. Hang pictures at eye level when you are standing. Arrange seating to make it easier for people to converse in small groups. You don't have to have expensive things to create an inviting space.

Fix What You Have

You may feel like replacing something because it is worn or because the color no longer suits you. Rather than just throwing it away, ask yourself whether there is something you can do to fix it up. Can you fix it by refinishing it? Or putting a new cover on it? Or painting it? We've somehow lost the art of repairing things in this country. But I believe that this is changing as we realize the impact our throwaway mentality has on the planet. Next time something breaks or is worn, try fixing it. It may take you several attempts before you know what you're doing, but you'll be amazed at your sense of accomplishment afterward.

Practice Routine Maintenance

In this era of cheap and disposable goods, we tend to be very quick about dumping our stuff. We say that we don't have time to practice maintenance. That our time is "too valuable" to spend maintaining our possessions. What we fail to consider is the time it takes for us to work to earn the money to buy new things.

By not maintaining our stuff, we also express our ingratitude for it. It's as if we will only take care of "good stuff" and not what we have. Unfortunately, that attitude can permeate our thinking, making us discontent with our lives.

Making the most of things that we already have is a way to practice gratitude on an everyday basis. Your contentment will be reflected in your attitude and in your orderly home.

• 49 •

Junk-Free Ways to Incorporate Beauty into Your Life

Beauty is important to our mental health. But sometimes we get confused and think that beauty is only found in things. Not true! If you are going to have an organized home, you must move beyond that way of thinking. Organization will automatically make things more attractive, and a beautiful space will entice you to keep it organized.

Function over Form

When given a choice between function or form, choose function. In an organized household, items that you have around need to work, not just look pretty. Remember that a well-functioning system can also be attractive.

Better Yet, Aim for Function and Form

That being said, while function *is* important, don't always go for the most utilitarian choice. Humans are naturally drawn to attractive and well-made items, whether it's a belt rack, an orange squeezer, or a file folder. I recently replaced my standard green Pendaflex folders with multicolored ones. I love them and have even gone so far as to show them to guests (they were thrilled). Do they make me more likely to file? You better believe it! (And I found a good home for my retired green folders, too.)

Incorporate Color

One way to incorporate beauty is to add splashes of color to everyday activities. Apple Computer started a revolution when they introduced computers that came in different colors. Soon, even staid computer companies who traditionally offered black or white were adding splashes of color to computer hardware. But office supplies are only the beginning. Color can be used in furnishings, to fix funky pieces you bought at yard sales (but not your antiques, please), or even outdoor furnishings. Color in unexpected places can dramatically add to the appearance of your home.

Remember Your Other Senses

We tend to think of beauty only in terms of what we can see. But our other senses appreciate beauty as well. For our sense of hearing, have wonderful music available. Similarly, beautiful writing is a feast for both eye and ear.

Good food is a treat for your mouth. Even simple bread, cheese, and fruit can be delightful. And now that you are well stocked with cutting boards and sharp knives, it will be a snap to prepare.

Beauty can also be experienced through touch. Have surfaces that are enjoyable to touch in your home, including a comfortable place for your entire family to be together. People love contrasting textures and surfaces that are pleasing to their hands. Finally, don't forget fragrance. Assuming no one has allergies, try to incorporate pleasant scents in your home. We relate to odors on a very visceral level, and attach emotionally to them. Certain scents will always say "home" to you and your family. Try to find ways to incorporate pleasant ones.

As you become more organized in your home and in your life, beauty will start naturally occurring. You can speed the process by paying attention to the details of your everyday life. You'll be happy you did.

• 50 •

Rome Wasn't Built in a Day
and Other Final Thoughts

As we come to a close, I want to leave you with some advice you can take with you on your organizational journey.

This May Take a While

Don't be discouraged if your organizational efforts take more than a weekend. It may actually take several weeks or even months before your home is organized. However, each step you take will move you closer to your goal. Here are some suggestions about how to tackle this big job.

Focus on areas you use every day. You might find that your efforts are better spent working on an area of your home that you use every day. So often, we begin our organizational odyssey by tackling the attic or garage. But we can work really hard in those spaces and not have them touch our everyday lives. On the other hand, if you try to organize your kitchen or bedroom, the impact will be immediate and will let you know that you are making progress.

Set reasonable goals. We often get discouraged from making life changes because we set impossible goals for ourselves. You might be tempted to promise that you will be organized "in a week." I hope you've learned by now to be more realistic. You're much less likely to become discouraged if you are regularly meeting goals. While you probably won't be able to organize your whole home in a week, you can probably fix your bathroom in that amount of time.

Provide yourself with rewards and incentives. I'm a firm believer in rewards for a job well done. As you meet goals you've set for yourself, provide a small reward. It could even be as simple as an hour off to enjoy a book, a day with friends, or a trip to the museum. Working all the time is no fun and isn't good for you. Intersperse your hard work with some fun and rewards along the way.

Don't expect to do things perfectly. As adults, we often labor under the belief that we should know how to do things the first time we attempt them. Rubbish! Make mistakes and learn from them. Realize you may not come up with the perfect solution the first time you try. Give yourself room to experiment. You might also find that you need to change things as the needs of your household change. The needs of a family with teens are different than a family with toddlers. Single people have different needs than couples. Be flexible.

Be kind to your friends. My final admonition, before I send you out into the world, is to be kind to your friends. As you become more organized, you may be tempted to share your newly found knowledge with others. My advice to you can be summed up in a single word—don't! When you are at someone's house and open a horror show of a drawer, shut it, slap your hand over your eyes, and repeat after me: "None of my business, none of my business." Don't offer assistance unless asked. No one likes an organizational cop. The golden rule applies here. Would you like someone doing this to you? Then *please* don't do it to others.

Well my friends, it's time to go. I know you are on your way to being more organized. Have a wonderful life and enjoy your organized home!

Resources

Aslett, Don. 1984. *Clutter's Last Stand*. Cincinnati, Ohio: Writer's Digest Books.

Bach, David. 2002. *Smart Couples Finish Rich*. Broadway: New York.

Dominguez, Joe, and Vicki Robin. 1992. *Your Money or Your Life: Transforming Your Relationship with Money and Achieving Financial Independence*. N.Y.: Viking.

Morgenstern, Julie. 1998. *Organizing from the Inside Out*. N.Y.: Owl Books.

National Sleep Foundation. 2000. *2000 Omnibus Sleep in America Poll*. www.sleepfoundation.org.

Organized Home.com. Lots of useful suggestions for cleaning clutter and becoming more organized.

Robinson, Jo, and Jean Coppock Staeheli. 1991. *Unplug the Christmas Machine*. Quill: New York.

Stoddard, Alexandra. 1988. *Living a Beautiful Life: 500 Ways to Add Elegance, Order, Beauty and Joy to Every Day of Your Life*. N.Y.: Morrow, William & Co.

———. 1992. *Creating a Beautiful Home*. N.Y.: Avon Books.

Kathleen Kendall-Tackett, Ph.D., is a health psychologist whose work involves helping people cope with the stresses and strains of daily life. A research associate at the Family Research Laboratory and a Research Associate Professor of Psychology at the University of New Hampshire, she is also a fellow of the American Psychological Association.

Kendall-Tackett has seen the impact of disorganization both in her own life, and in the lives of families she knows. While in graduate school, she had numerous housecleaning and homemaking jobs. It is the combination of her research interests and her life experiences that led her to understand the psychological stress people experience when confronted with chronic disorganization and to formulate her unique insights into the simple techniques that can transform a home from a clutter zone into a clean and serene place.

Some Other New Harbinger Titles

Sex Talk, Item SEXT $12.95

Everyday Adventures for the Soul, Item EVER $11.95

A Woman's Addiction Workbook, Item $18.95

The Daughter-In-Law's Survival Guide, Item DSG $12.95

PMDD, Item PMDD $13.95

The Vulvodynia Survival Guide, Item VSG $15.95

Love Tune-Ups, Item LTU $10.95

The Deepest Blue, Item DPSB $13.95

The 50 Best Ways to Simplify Your Life, Item FWSL $11.95

Brave New You, Item BVNY $13.95

Loving Your Teenage Daughter, Item LYTD $14.95

The Hidden Feelings of Motherhood, Item HFM $14.95

The Woman's Book of Sleep, Item WBS $14.95

Pregnancy Stories, Item PS $14.95

The Women's Guide to Total Self-Esteem, Item WGTS $13.95

Thinking Pregnant, Item TKPG $13.95

The Conscious Bride, Item CB $12.95

Juicy Tomatoes, Item JTOM $13.95

Facing 30, Item F30 $12.95

The Money Mystique, Item MYST $13.95

Call **toll free, 1-800-748-6273,** or log on to our online bookstore at **www.newharbinger.com** to order. Have your Visa or Mastercard number ready. Or send a check for the titles you want to New Harbinger Publications, Inc., 5674 Shattuck Ave., Oakland, CA 94609. Include $4.50 for the first book and 75¢ for each additional book, to cover shipping and handling. (California residents please include appropriate sales tax.) Allow two to five weeks for delivery.

Prices subject to change without notice.